Companion to

Macbeth

Patrick Murray

THE EDUCATIONAL COMPANY

First published 1985
This reprint 1993

The paper used in
this book comes
from Managed
Forests in
Northern
Europe
For
every
tree
felled, at
least one new
tree is planted

The Educational Company of Ireland
Ballymount Road
Walkinstown
Dublin 12

A trading unit of Smurfit Services Limited

Design and Typesetting by Phototype-Set Ltd, Glasnevin, Dublin.
Proofreading: Clodagh Brook

Printed in the Republic of Ireland by
Citiprint Ltd., Dublin.
       2   3   4   5   6   7   8   9

Contents

Scene-by-scene Analysis and Commentary

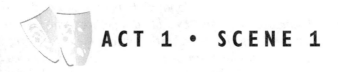 **ACT 1 • SCENE 1**

*In an open place, swept by a thunderstorm, three Witches
appear. They discuss their impending meeting with Macbeth,
which will follow a decisive battle. Accompanied by their
familiars or companions, demons in animal form, they depart
through the foggy air.*

COMMENTARY

SHORT as this scene is, it contributes some significant details. The
thunder and lightning of the stage-direction are symbolic of the moral
and spiritual confusion and tumult soon to overtake Macbeth. The power of
the Witches to control the elements is suggested in the first two lines. The
two opening questions posed by the Witches imply that they are able to
determine the kind of weather that will prevail at their next meeting. Their
gift of prophecy is underlined in the answers of the Second and Third
Witches to the routine questions of the First. They know in advance that
they are going to meet with Macbeth upon the heath, after the battle and
before sunset. Their sinister significance and intentions are conveyed in the
closing two lines of the scene. Their favourite element is the filthy air
obscured by fog, another symbol of the confusion they represent and create.
Their paradoxical slogan, 'Fair is foul, and foul is fair', is a neat summary of
their reversal of all moral values. It is a point of view that is to be soon
embraced by the two main characters in the play. Graymalkin and Paddock
who call to the Witches are their familiars or companions, usually identified
as a cat and a toad. The toad was considered to be poisonous as well as ugly,
and so has a symbolic function here.

ACT 1 • SCENE 2

Duncan, king of Scotland, and his sons, Malcolm and
Donalbain, are confronted by a bleeding officer, who has just
come from the scene of a fierce battle between the royal forces led
by the king's cousin Macbeth and a rebel army of traitors led by
Macdonwald. Macbeth has defeated the rebels and slain
Macdonwald, but is locked in another conflict with the forces of
the king of Norway. Ross enters to report that the king of
Norway and his treacherous ally the Thane of Cawdor have
been defeated by Macbeth and Banquo.

COMMENTARY

THE chief purpose of this scene is to provide information about
Macbeth as a warrior and, to a lesser extent, about Banquo. The
emphasis, whether we consider the visual impact of a profusely bleeding
officer coming onstage, or the verbal images of the battle, is on blood and
slaughter. Two equally strong impressions of Macbeth are conveyed here.
One is his heroic performance in battle. Both the bleeding Captain and
Ross emphasise Macbeth's bravery, which extends far beyond the demands
of duty. He is 'brave Macbeth', 'with Valour armed', acquitting himself like
another Mars ('Bellona's bridegroom') on the battlefield, saving his king
and country from the grasp of traitors and rebels, as well as repelling
invaders. But there is another, disturbing, side to the energetic account of
Macbeth's military achievements. His valour is tinged with what appears
like a barbaric enjoyment of slaughter for its own sake. In the titanic
battle with Macdonwald's men, he has 'carved out his passage' through a
host of enemies and 'unseemed' their chief, ripping him open from the
stomach upwards. This ferocity is part of Macbeth's nature, and will come
to the fore again in his dealings with his various victims. Initially, however, he will be most reluctant to display it against Duncan.

ACT 1 • SCENE 3

*The Witches discuss the various kinds of harm they can
cause to human beings. A drum beat heralds the arrival of
Macbeth and Banquo. Macbeth is hailed by the Witches as
Thane of Glamis and of Cawdor, and as future king of Scotland.
Banquo is greeted as the begetter of kings. The Witches vanish,
and the truth of one of their prophecies is confirmed when Ross
gives Macbeth the news that the king has made him Thane of
Cawdor. Banquo warns Macbeth against the dangers posed by
occult powers. Macbeth in soliloquy reveals his troubled mind.*

COMMENTARY

THE first scene was devoted exclusively to the Witches and the second
to human beings. This scene brings the two together. In the first scene
the Witches seemed impressive enough. Here they inspire somewhat less
fear and little confidence in their power to do harm. Their malicious deeds
have a slightly childish quality. The Second Witch has killed swine
apparently because their owner annoyed her. The First Witch came across
a sailor's wife who refused to hand over some chestnuts. By way of
reprisal, the Witch does her utmost to harm the woman's husband. Her
efforts in this direction, however, do not say very much for her capacity to
harm. She has power over the winds, but cannot destroy the unnamed
sailor ('Though his bark cannot be lost,/Yet it shall be tempest-tost'). Her
production of the shipwrecked pilot's thumb scarcely marks her as a
serious or dedicated agent of supernatural evil.

Macbeth is a play full of echoes and anticipations. An example is the
passage beginning 'I'll drain him dry as hay'. This passage is about the
master of the *Tiger*, but most of it can also be read as a comment on
Macbeth's fate. Like the anonymous sailor, Macbeth will be 'drained',
though morally and spiritually rather than physically. He will also be
deprived of sleep (3, 2, 17-22). Macbeth, too, will be cursed and ostracised
('a man forbid'), and will 'dwindle, peak and pine' (see 5, 2, 20-2). The most
significant lines of the First Witch's speech are: 'Though his bark cannot

be lost,/Yet it shall be tempest-tost'. The worst the Witches can do to the master of the *Tiger* is to cause the winds to buffet his ship, but he keeps control of his destiny in spite of their utmost efforts. These lines cannot be applied directly to Macbeth, since his 'bark' (his cause, his life, his body, his soul) *is* lost. But the reason for this is that Macbeth will not fight sufficiently hard to resist the destructive forces of temptation. He is partly the agent of his own destruction, unlike the master of the *Tiger*, who will not scuttle his ship. The fate of the pilot, 'Wracked as homeward he did come', is an ironic anticipation of what will happen to Macbeth as he makes his way homeward after the battle.

From the point of view of characterisation, the most interesting feature of this scene is found in the contrasting attitudes of Banquo and Macbeth to the pronouncements of the Witches. As Banquo points out to him, Macbeth ought to respond with pleasure to the prophecies. Instead, he is startled and fearful. When the Witches predict a royal crown for him, they nowhere suggest that he should get it by foul means. Macbeth's guilty start reflects guilty thoughts already formed. The Witches are merely encouraging Macbeth to do something he has previously been tempted to do. The idea of killing Duncan for his crown has clearly occurred to him before his encounter with the Witches. If this were not the case, it would indeed be difficult to account for the vivid and terrifying images of murder in his soliloquy.

Banquo's response to the Witches and what they have to say is quite different from Macbeth's in some important respects. His feelings are far less deeply engaged. He is rather sceptical about the significance of their prophecies, and is conscious that evil spirits can bring about the downfall of men by tempting them initially with 'honest trifles'. Macbeth knows this as well as Banquo, but chooses to ignore it because he wants what the Witches promise him. Banquo has comparatively little regard for whatever good or ill the Witches may intend for him (their 'favours' or their 'hate'). Macbeth is passionately interested, and wants to know from what superior authority the Witches have derived their information ('this strange intelligence'). It is Macbeth, not Banquo, who wants to discuss the matter further ('let us speak/Our free hearts each to other'). When Macbeth hears the predictions for his own future, he wants to learn more; Banquo does not bother to make further enquiries. It is significant that Macbeth takes refuge in untruth to conceal his intense interest in what he has heard, pretending that his 'dull brain was wrought/With things forgotten', when, in fact, he has obviously been meditating not on the past but on the future.

ACT 1 • SCENE 4

Malcolm gives Duncan details of Cawdor's execution.
Duncan thanks Macbeth for his services to king and country, is
fulsomely answered, and then formally makes his son Malcolm
successor to the throne. Macbeth responds to this unwelcome
news in an aside which reveals his murderous plans.

COMMENTARY

THE first Thane of Cawdor is praised here by Malcolm for ending his rebellious life on a good note. The main point of the reference to Cawdor is to suggest a contrast between the good ending of the first Cawdor's career and the bad beginning of that of Macbeth, the second Cawdor.

Duncan's commonplace generalisation about the difficulty of deducing the true nature of man from his outward appearance becomes deeply ironic as Macbeth enters. Duncan is regretting the trust he reposed in Cawdor, but is at the same time ready to trust his 'worthiest cousin', and to reward him lavishly. In the light of what we know of Macbeth's intentions towards Duncan, everything the latter says by way of praise and gratitude is full of irony, some of it particularly ominous and sinister, as when Duncan tells his potential murderer that 'More is thy due than more than all can pay', not realising that the 'more than all' will be his own life. To the end of the scene, Duncan is the vehicle for further ironies of that kind. It is appropriate that a scene so remarkable for its ironies should end on an ironic note. Duncan's last words are a tribute to his 'peerless kinsman', Macbeth.

The contrasts between the style and tone of Duncan's speeches and those of Macbeth in this scene are worth noting. Duncan is full of joyful enthusiasm which he expresses without restraint; he sometimes becomes embarrassingly sentimental ('My plenteous joys,/Wanton in fulness, seek to hide themselves/In drops of sorrow'). Macbeth's replies are forced, formal and conventional, reflecting his inability to pretend he can share in Duncan's happiness. The turning-point of the scene, and one of the crucial moments of the play, is Duncan's proud and happy nomination of his son Malcolm as his successor. It is this gesture that, more than anything else, seals his doom. Macbeth's public response to the announcement is curt and ironic: he will make Lady Macbeth 'joyful' with the news that Duncan is to visit them. His short aside just before the end of the scene is full of menace. Duncan has been talking of titles and honours shining 'like stars' on all who deserve them. Macbeth looks to the extinction of the stars as a prelude to his murderous deed.

ACT 1 • SCENE 5

*Lady Macbeth reads her husband's letter conveying the
news of the Witches' prophecies. In her analysis of Macbeth's
character, she is worried by the thought that he may lack the
necessary ruthlessness to take the crown. The announcement of
the imminent visit of Duncan to her castle excites her to near
hysteria. She invokes the aid of evil spirits to strengthen her
resolution and harden her heart. Macbeth is unsure of what to
do. Lady Macbeth is resolved that Duncan must die.*

COMMENTARY

IN Act 1, Scene 2, we learned about Macbeth's qualities as a professional
soldier. In this scene we are given an intimate glimpse of Macbeth the
private man, first through the medium of his letter to Lady Macbeth, and
then in her significant comments on his character, in soliloquy. Another
major function of this scene is to throw light on Lady Macbeth's character
and motives.

Her speech beginning 'Glamis thou art, and Cawdor' is a major piece
of evidence about Macbeth's character from the person who, presumably,
knows him best. Lady Macbeth's purpose is to indicate her husband's
weaknesses. Like the Witches, however, she has a perverted sense of
moral values. For them, 'Fair is foul, and foul is fair'. For her, compassion,
scrupulousness, humane feeling and integrity are to be deplored in a man
who wants to get on in the world. She sees it as her function to overcome
these 'defects' in his character by pouring her 'spirits' in his ear, by
infecting him with a ruthless inhumanity.

Her next speech, particularly the invocation of the spirits (*l.* 39 *ff.*)
must be understood in terms of contemporary theories of witchcraft and
demonology. In this passage, Lady Macbeth is formally and deliberately
dedicating herself to evil spirits, asking them to possess her, body and
soul. She is assuming the role of a witch. If we accept this, a good deal of

what she says and does, and of what happens all around her, falls into place. Her prayer to the powers of evil is not an empty, conventional formula. Some of the great interpreters of the role of Lady Macbeth have recognised the terrible implications of what Shakespeare has in mind here. The actress Mrs Siddons, the most famous of all Lady Macbeths, declared that 'having imperiously delivered herself up to the excitements of hell, Lady Macbeth is abandoned to the guidance of the demons she has invoked'. A contemporary critic reported that Mrs Siddons spoke the invocation in a slow hollow whisper, that her voice sounded quite supernatural, as in a horrible dream, and that the rhythms of the speech made the blood run cold. Irene Worth, one of the best modern actresses to play the part, saw Lady Macbeth's speech in much the same way. Kenneth Tynan reports that she spoke her great petition 'not as a bombastic verbal gesture but as a straightforward request, addressed to a supernatural authority that is perfectly capable of answering it'.

The clause 'That tend on mortal thoughts' (*l.* 40) has a deep significance for students of demonology. 'Tend on' means 'wait on' or 'attend on'. The evil spirits wait for evidence of evil thoughts ('mortal thoughts' are thoughts of murder), because such thoughts will allow them to take possession of the minds and wills of those who harbour them. What Lady Macbeth does here is to *will* the evil spirits to take possession of her, so that she may become a more effective agent of 'mortal' or murderous deeds. The 'murdering ministers' of line 47 are the same as the 'spirits' of line 39.

If we think of the demonic spirits as having taken possession of Lady Macbeth, we shall not find it surprising that the Porter of Inverness thinks of himself as letting people into hell when he opens the gate of her home. The influence of these spirits is also felt in the unnatural portents on the night of Duncan's murder (Act 2, Scene 4), and in the unnatural darkness surrounding the castle ('There's husbandry in heaven;/Their candles are all out', Act 2, Scene 1, *ll.* 4-5). In his classic study of the subject, the critic W. C. Curry points out that one of the characteristics of demonical sleepwalking was that a second personality spoke through the victim's mouth, confessing sins and recalling earlier episodes from his or her life. Whether the 'damned spot' (5, 1, 31) is the devil's mark traditionally supposed to be found on a witch is uncertain, but Lady Macbeth's behaviour during the sleepwalking scene, and Macbeth's behaviour at other times (when he sees the phantom dagger and when

Banquo's ghost appears) illustrates the traditional belief that 'demons are enabled to induce in the imaginations of men, either waking or asleep, whatever visions or hallucinations they please' (W. C. Curry, *Shakespeare's Philosophical Patterns*, 1937, p. 75). Two references to Lady Macbeth make explicit the idea that she is possessed. 'More needs she the divine than the physician' (5, 1, 66), says the Doctor, the exorcism of evil spirits being one of the functions of a priest. And she is finally described by Malcolm as Macbeth's 'fiend-like queen' (5, 9, 35).

Lady Macbeth's dealings with the powers of evil may be contrasted with Banquo's. He cannot keep himself from dreaming of the Witches, but he prays, not to Lady Macbeth's 'spirits / 'That tend on mortal thoughts', but instead to the 'Merciful Powers' (2, 1, 7). Here he is not making a vague appeal to heaven for help against temptation. The 'Powers' he invokes are those good angels whose task it is to restrain and counteract evil spirits. Banquo's will, at this point at any rate, controls his 'cursed thoughts'. Lady Macbeth's, by contrast, has fostered hers. She remains powerfully effective as long as her conscious mind remains in control. But even her will cannot control her unconscious mind, and it is from this source that her final collapse comes. When she admits that a resemblance between her father and the sleeping Duncan prevented her from killing the latter, she betrays her one conscious weakness in the play and her one notable streak of human feeling.

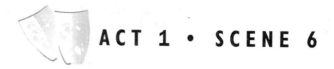

ACT 1 • SCENE 6

*Duncan, accompanied by his courtiers, arrives at
Macbeth's castle, and is greeted with fulsome expressions of
courtesy and flattery by Lady Macbeth.*

COMMENTARY

THIS is a gentle, peaceful scene, suggesting an unruffled calm before a great storm. The speeches of Duncan and Banquo feature images of fruitful natural life and order, the kind of order Macbeth and Lady Macbeth reject in their speeches and deeds. Irony predominates throughout. The chief victim, Duncan, enters the place of his execution full of praise for the beauty of its setting and surroundings. He compliments the chief architect of his murder. She in turn is eloquently convincing in her protestations of loyalty to her victim. Her mention of their 'service' to Duncan, of the 'honours deep and broad wherewith/Your Majesty loads our house', is touched with its own macabre irony. She is certainly much more accomplished at concealing her real feelings and intentions than Macbeth appeared to be in the similar circumstances of Act 1, Scene 4. Duncan's position as the pathetic victim of deceitful appearance is underlined to the very end. He interprets Macbeth's haste in reaching the castle before him as a sign of great love. The irony of Duncan's situation is visually expressed at the close of the scene when Lady Macbeth leads him by the hand into the castle and to his doom.

ACT 1 • SCENE 7

Macbeth detaches himself from the company, and displays much confusion of mind and spirit over the plan to murder Duncan. By the time Lady Macbeth joins him, he has decided not to proceed. In a remarkable exercise of will, she overcomes his doubts and scruples.

COMMENTARY

THE scene opens with Macbeth's remarkable soliloquy. Here he analyses the implications, for himself, of the murder he is contemplating. What is most significant about this speech is its clear analysis of the reality behind what he is about to do, its frank acknowledgement of the evil involved in the murder of the king. Not even Macbeth's worst enemies could come up with a more powerful condemnation of his deed than the one he himself sets out here. He gives all the right reasons for not proceeding to kill Duncan: such deeds, he knows, tend even in this life to plague those who perform them; Duncan is his relative as well as his anointed king; he will be violating the sacred laws of hospitality if he kills the man he should be protecting against harm; Duncan has been a just and good king, and heaven will cry out in condemnation of his murder. Against such overwhelming reasons for not killing Duncan, he can think of only one reason for carrying out the deed: an inordinate ambition of the kind that often leads to disaster. This soliloquy is a splendidly-reasoned argument against the murder. It closes on a note of irony with Macbeth telling himself that ambition is his only 'spur'. With the entry of Lady Macbeth, he has another spur to goad him on, as we soon discover.

The part of the scene following this soliloquy is of critical importance, since what happens in it launches Macbeth firmly on the path of self-destruction. Lady Macbeth is the active agent throughout this scene (note her dominance again in the banquet scene). Macbeth's defences against her varied assaults are hopelessly inadequate; the chief dramatic interest in the scene is her brilliant deployment of her great resources of will against her weaker partner. The nature of her triumph is illustrated in the short time that elapses (only fifty lines of dialogue) between Macbeth's determination to 'proceed no further in this business', and 'I am settled, and bend up/Each corporal agent to this terrible feat'. It is interesting to watch her at work as she batters down his defences one by one. Lady Macbeth's arguments, all in the form of rebukes, are of four kinds: her husband is changeable and lacking in resolution (*ll.* 35-8); his love for her is not what she thought it was if he will not do this much for her *(ll.* 38-9); his determination is no better than that of a drunkard, 'green and pale' after a hangover *(ll.* 37-9); he lacks courage and manliness *(ll.* 39-54). The last rebuke is her most effective, because the most deeply wounding, method of attack, since courage and physical prowess are Macbeth's major claims to self-esteem and public respect; without them he is nothing. Her cries of 'coward'; 'poor cat'; 'then you were a man'; 'you would/Be so much more the man', ring in his ears until resistance is no longer possible. The turning-point in the scene, and in the play, comes with his words, 'If we should fail?' (*l.* 59).

Up to this, Macbeth's counter-arguments have been moral ones: he doesn't want to show base ingratitude to his recent benefactor who has so honoured him (*l.* 32); the deed would be unworthy of a human being (*ll.* 46-7). But now Lady Macbeth has succeeded in transferring the argument from the moral plane to that of mere expediency and planning. Macbeth has given in on principle. All that remains for her to do is to suggest some practical scheme — or at least one that will temporarily convince him — and he will be ready to proceed. Her plan is not a very convincing one, and would scarcely pass muster in real life. His enthusiastic comments on it (*ll.* 72-7) are almost simple-minded; that he can accept such a plan and even admire it shows the extent of his submission and mental captivity at this point. His 'Bring forth men-children only!' (*l.* 72) is an endorsement of her ideas on 'manliness' (*ll.* 39-54).

The scene has many echoes and anticipations of other parts of the play. The clothing image which Macbeth uses to express pride in his newly-won honours ('Golden opinions . . . worn now in their newest gloss . . . cast aside') is one of a series beginning with his incredulous 'why do you dress me/In borrowed robes?' (1, 3, 108-9), and culminating in the picture of kingship as 'a giant's robe/Upon a dwarfish thief' (5, 2, 21-2). Lady Macbeth sarcastically takes up the clothing image in one of Shakespeare's most astonishing mixed metaphors, reminding her husband that he had dressed himself in the garments of hope as well as those of 'Golden opinions', and that the former garments now seem in a sorry state (as well as looking like a newly-awakened drunkard!). The references to 'act and valour' (*l.* 40) on the one hand, and 'desire' (*l.* 41) on the other, are often paralleled elsewhere. In this scene we are made vividly aware of a great gap between Macbeth's desire to be king and his willingness to act in order to make himself so. Later, the gap is closed. He will seal the fate of Macduff's family with: 'Strange things I have in head that will to hand,/Which must be acted ere they may be scanned' (3, 4, 139-40).

The lines 'What beast was't then/That made you break this enterprise to me?' (*ll.* 47-8) have been the subject of much editorial comment. It is clear that the dramatic force of 'beast' lies in its powerful juxtaposition with 'man' in lines 46 and 49-51. Macbeth wants to be a man, not the subhuman brute which murdering Duncan would make him; what subhuman force then, his wife asks, made him discuss with her the possibility of the murder? Most of the critical debate has centred on the significance of 'break this enterprise', which seems to suggest that Macbeth has already talked of the murder to her. Since there is no sign of this in the text as we have it, it is possible that Lady Macbeth is referring to the contents of his letter (1, 5, 1-13), and is now reading more into it, for her own purposes, than is actually there. We must remember that people arguing excitedly, as she is doing here, often go beyond the facts of the situation in order to make their point.

Lady Macbeth's reference to her child (*ll.* 54-9) has often been interpreted to suggest that she is a totally unnatural and unwomanly creature. She has, it is true, prayed to be filled with 'direst cruelty' and to be freed from all 'remorse' (1, 5, 42-3). It has already been suggested that she is to be seen, after this invocation, as the willing victim of demoniacal possession (see commentary on Act I, Scene 5). But the passage about the child cannot be used as further evidence for this. Indeed, far from suggesting that she is unnaturally cruel, it may readily be interpreted in the opposite sense. Coleridge's comment on the matter is worth quoting: 'Had she so sworn, she would have done that which was most horrible to her feelings, rather than break the oath; and as the most horrible act which it was possible for the imagination to conceive, as that which was most revolting to her own feelings, she alludes to the destruction of her infant. Had she regarded this with savage indifference, there would have been no force in the appeal; but her very allusion to it, and her purpose in this allusion, showed that she considered no tie so tender as that which connected her with her babe.'

ACT 2 • SCENE 1

Banquo enters the dark courtyard with his son Fleance.
Macbeth's entry is heralded by a servant with a torch. There is
some polite but uneasy discussion between Macbeth and
Banquo about their future prospects and their relationship.
Macbeth sends a servant to arrange for the ringing of the bell as
a signal that all is in readiness for the murder. Alone, Macbeth
has a vision of a dagger, draws his own to test the vision against
the reality, and then imagines his visionary dagger covered with
blood. The vision fades, and Macbeth prepares himself for his
murderous task, moving towards the king's bedchamber as the
bell rings.

COMMENTARY

THE scene begins on a note of foreboding. The starless night has a symbolic significance: the world is given over to the powers of darkness. Banquo has been troubled by cursed dreams. The relationship between Macbeth and Banquo seems no longer quite that of loyal comrades or friends. Banquo is on his guard, sword at the ready, in a place where he should feel a secure and honoured guest. He acts like a sentinel on duty, and challenges Macbeth ('Who's there?') in Macbeth's own castle. The latter responds to the incongruous challenge without, apparently, noticing anything odd. Their discussion of their meeting with the Weird Sisters is inconclusive. Macbeth is less than honest in his comments; Banquo dismisses the notion that Macbeth might be tempted to gain advancement at the expense of his (Banquo's) honour.

It is clear from this scene that Banquo, like Macbeth, has been disturbed by what the Witches have promised. But his response is to struggle manfully against whatever temptations beset him as a result. He calls on the 'Merciful Powers', those spirits assigned by God to restrain demons, to protect him from giving way to evil thoughts. Macbeth and

Lady Macbeth, on the other hand, will enlist the aid of evil powers in pursuing their aims. Macbeth's imagination and his conscience have already told him emphatically what he must not do. His failure is to lie in his lack of will to follow the promptings of his imagination and conscience. Banquo, on the other hand, has the will to avoid what he knows is wrong, and to seek supernatural aid in doing so.

The dagger soliloquy is important for the impression it conveys of Macbeth's state of mind just before the murder of Duncan. The phantom dagger is not to be regarded as an additional temptation, since it is clear from the soliloquy that Macbeth has already decided on the murder. When he says that the dagger is marshalling him 'the way that I was going', he is imagining the dagger pointing towards Duncan's room; he is also conscious of the fact that the dagger is indicating a deed that he has already decided on.

ACT 2 • SCENE 2

*A tense, distraught Lady Macbeth comes into the
courtyard. Macbeth, carrying the daggers in bloodstained
hands, returns from the scene of his crime, to undergo
questioning from his wife. He becomes increasingly hysterical;
she acts as a calming influence. A knocking on the gate poses a
new threat. She deals with this by telling him to appear as if he
has just risen from sleep.*

COMMENTARY

THE murder of Duncan is enacted offstage. The tact that we do not
actually *see* Macbeth killing Duncan is significant; it inevitably makes
the deed less appalling to the feelings and to the imagination than it
would otherwise have been.

The chief interest of the scene is not in the murder itself but in the
reactions of the two main characters to it. Even Lady Macbeth is nervous
and uncertain. She is momentarily startled by a shriek, which turns out to
be the cry of an owl. As Macbeth calls out, she fears that something has
gone seriously wrong with their plans.

Macbeth's horrified response to what he has done unsettles and
disturbs his wife further. As he looks at his 'hangman's hands' he loses
control. His outbursts of self-reproach become hysterical, and leave his
more practical, rational, calculating wife at a loss. She can only plead for a
reasonable approach to what has been done ('Consider it not so deeply . . .
so, it will make us mad'). She pleads in vain. Her efforts are so concen-
trated on calming the tempest in his mind that it takes her quite a time to
notice that he has carried the daggers with him from the scene of the
crime. Her suggestion that 'A little water clears us of this deed' is one of
the many powerful ironies of the play, an irony echoed in the sleepwalking
scene, (Act 5, Scene 1), when we find her wondering if her hands will ever
be clean again. As she goes back to Duncan's chamber with the daggers,

Macbeth is still overwhelmed by guilt and remorse. She, the practical one, has to rouse him from his trance, if they are to face those who are knocking so insistently at the gate.

The contrast here between the two chief characters is remarkable. Macbeth's uncontrolled outbursts of anguish make him appear indifferent to his fate and leave him open to detection. He has committed the murder in a kind of trance, and has neglected even the most basic precautions against detection. It is left to Lady Macbeth to take care of such vital practical details as leaving the daggers back in the bedchamber, and making sure that she and Macbeth will not appear as if they have been up and about at the dead of night ('Get on your nightgown, lest occasion call us/And show us to be watchers' *ll.* 71-2).

ACT 2 • SCENE 3

*In response to continued knocking on the gate, a drunken
porter admits Macduff and Lennox. Macbeth greets them, and
talks to Lennox while Macduff goes straight to Duncan's
chamber. Seeing what has happened, he calls in horror for the
alarm-bell to be sounded. Macbeth tells Malcolm and
Donalbain of their father's death, and reports that he himself
has slain the grooms in a fit of vengeance. Lady Macbeth faints,
and Malcolm and Donalbain make plans to flee the country.*

COMMENTARY

THE Porter episode which opens this scene cannot be regarded simply
as comic relief, nor is there any need to dismiss it as a piece of
nonsense unworthy of Shakespeare and inserted by actors. Its inclusion in
the play can be defended on theatrical grounds, since there has to be a
scene between Macbeth's exit and Macduff's entry. The last few lines of
Act 2, Scene 2 make it clear that Macbeth must change his clothes and
wash his hands. The old idea that the scene was inserted by Shakespeare
to provide comic relief is no longer taken seriously. For one thing, it would
be difficult to see why Shakespeare would have introduced a lighthearted
episode merely to dissipate the tension he had steadily built up in the
previous nine scenes.

The images and themes of the Porter's speeches are part of a pattern
extending through much of the play. His talk of hell and the devil, for
example, appears singularly appropriate against the background of the
evil forces at work in the castle, and particularly in the light of Lady
Macbeth's self-dedication to evil in Act 1, Scene 5. The Porter's references
to the equivocator's treason remind us of Cawdor's betrayal of his country,
and are, in turn, echoed in Macbeth's equivocal answers to Lennox and
Macduff on his next appearance. Equivocation is to become an important
theme in the play. Macbeth is led on to his doom when the Witches give
him 'earnest of success,/Commencing in a truth' (1, 3, 132-3). At the end
he will have every reason to 'doubt th'equivocation of the fiend,/That lies

like truth' (5, 5, 43-4). Again, the Porter's images of the farmer and the tailor may be related to the images drawn from natural growth and clothing, which recur throughout the play.

With the exit of the Porter, the focus of attention shifts to Macbeth. There is much significance in the brevity of his replies and comments to Macduff and Lennox. He says as little as he can ('Good morrow, both . . . Not yet . . . I'll bring you to him'). To account for this economy of words on Macbeth's part, we must consider his state of mind. Everything he says in these circumstances will involve deceit and equivocation, which can only intensify his already extreme suffering, and make him feel even worse about what he has done. His guilty conscience betrays itself in his quick correction of his own answer to the question put to him by Lennox about Duncan's plans to leave Inverness: 'He does: he did appoint so'.

The discovery of Duncan's murder comes as a relief to Macbeth, since he is then able to speak more freely and more eloquently, and actually mean what he is saying: 'Had I but died an hour before this chance/I had lived a blessed time'. In this most moving speech he is condemning himself, whether consciously or unconsciously; he is also saying things to which all his hearers must subscribe. His eloquent explanation of the killing of the grooms is cunningly devised. (The murder of the grooms marks yet another step in Macbeth's moral decline. Note that these are the first murders which he plans and executes without consulting with his 'partner', Lady Macbeth.

It is difficult to know exactly how one should interpret Lady Macbeth's fainting-fit. One explanation is that she stages it in order to draw attention away from her husband, because she fears that he may betray both of them in some rash outburst. Against this, it is sometimes argued that her fainting is all too genuine, the earliest hint that the strain of events is beginning to prove too great for her.

Banquo's silent role in much of this scene nevertheless gives some scope to the actor playing the part. Much can be suggested by the way in which he looks at Macbeth as the latter makes his self-justifying speeches. Banquo's two main interventions in the scene are impressive. One is a sharp rebuke to Lady Macbeth, following her expression of concern that Duncan should have been murdered in *her* home ('Too cruel anywhere' is Banquo's comment). The other is a firm and unequivocal commitment to the cause of right ('In the great hand of God I stand, . . .'). Later in the play, however, there will be reason to question the strength of Banquo's determination here to fight against 'the undivulged pretence' of treason.

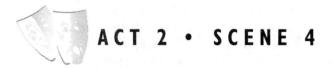 # ACT 2 • SCENE 4

*It is day, but the sky is unnaturally dark. Ross and the
Old Man discuss and interpret the strange omens which have
accompanied Duncan's death. Macduff, unlike Ross, will not go
to Scone for Macbeth's coronation.*

COMMENTARY

THIS scene takes us outside the main action. The Old Man and Ross act as commentators on the unnatural events that have accompanied Macbeth's unnatural deed. The two participants in this commentary are a nicely contrasted pair. The Old Man is superstitious and relatively simple-minded. His language is natural and sincere. Ross speaks an artificial and affected language. The references by each to the upheavals in nature are intended to reflect the common belief that violent disorder in the world of man (the murder of a king, for example) was bound to be reflected in some parallel disorder in the natural world. It would be a mistake to take such parallels too literally: Macbeth is not being compared to a mousing owl or Duncan to a falcon.

There is another instance of contrast in characterisation here, this time between Ross and Macduff. Ross accepts the 'official' story that the princes have killed their father, and he goes off to attend Macbeth's coronation. Macduff has his reservations. He will go home to Fife, and his parting words to Ross indicate his fears for the future of Scotland under Macbeth's leadership.

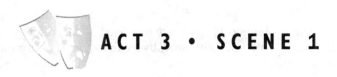

ACT 3 • SCENE 1

Banquo expresses his suspicions of Macbeth, but entertains his own hopes. Macbeth reminds him not to forget the feast at which he will be the chief guest, and then discovers, by means of innocent-sounding questions, where and how far Banquo will ride. Macbeth sends for Banquo's murderers and motivates them.

COMMENTARY

MACBETH is given no time to enjoy the fruits of Duncan's murder. The first small threat to his security has already been hinted at in the previous scene. Macduff is not happy with the course of events. In the present scene, Banquo voices *his* doubts about Macbeth, in soliloquy, suspecting that foul play has brought him to the throne. Banquo's own position appears to be somewhat ambiguous. He derives consolation, perhaps even guilty hope, from the thought that the Witches have predicted good fortune for him too, even though he has earlier warned Macbeth about believing in the promises of the 'instruments of darkness'.

Macbeth's first words in this scene ('Here's our chief guest') sound sinister in view of what has happened to his earlier chief guest, Duncan. This scene presents us with a Macbeth who is much changed from the conscience-stricken, terrified figure of Act 2, appalled by his own guilt and given over to outbursts of moral hysteria. Here we see him as a cunning hypocrite, coldly calculating and untroubled by conscience. He displays much deviousness in eliciting all the information he needs from his intended victim in order to arrange the details of Banquo's and Fleance's murder. The key questions ('Ride you this afternoon? . . . Is't far you ride? . . . Goes Fleance with you?') are so innocuously placed that Banquo's suspicions are not aroused.

Banquo, too, wears a mask. He displays the outward marks of loyalty and respect for his new king, stressing the 'indissoluble tie' between himself and his 'good lord' Macbeth. The latter savours the irony of his direction to Banquo to 'Fail not our feast'. The irony of Banquo's reply, 'My lord, I will not' will be fully realised in the tumult of the banquet scene (Act 3, Scene 4).

Macbeth's soliloquy on Banquo ('To be thus is nothing,. . . utterance!') resembles his earlier one on Duncan ('If it were done, when 'tis done'). In each case, tribute is paid to the good and noble qualities of the victims: here we learn of Banquo's regal nature, his bravery and his wisdom. This time, however, Macbeth abandons logic. The Witches have proved totally accurate in his own case: he has become Thane of Cawdor and king. But in this meditation he thinks he can prove the Witches false by killing Banquo and Fleance. At the conclusion of the soliloquy he is challenging fate.

Macbeth's conference with the murderers marks a further degeneration of his character. His nobility and sensitivity give way to cunning, double-dealing and hypocrisy. He appeals to whatever self-esteem the murderers may have by implying that they are particularly well qualified to carry out this mission. He has learned a good deal from Lady Macbeth. In urging her husband to commit his first crime, she appealed above all to his sense of manliness, and her appeal proved decisive. Now he is appealing to the same quality in the murderers ('if you have a station in the file,/Not i'the worst rank of manhood, say it' 3, 1, 102-3).

ACT 3 • SCENE 2

Lady Macbeth sends for her husband. She is weary and disillusioned. Macbeth is neither happy nor secure. He has murderous business in hand which he will not reveal to her until after it has been completed.

COMMENTARY

THIS domestic scene reveals the insecurity and unhappiness of Macbeth and his wife, and marks a deterioration in the quality of their relationship. Her suffering and turmoil are evident from her pathetically brief soliloquy ('Nought's had, all's spent'). She will not, however, let Macbeth know the full extent of her misery. She deflects attention from this by rebuking him for his gloomy mood (his 'sorriest fancies') and advising him to accept the inevitable ('what's done is done'). Macbeth's speech ('We have scorched the snake') is an unconscious echo of his wife's soliloquy; he, too, is suffering the torments of the damned ('terrible dreams . . . torture of the mind . . . restless ecstasy'). Like her, he envies the peaceful sleep of the dead.

What is most significant here is the change in the relationship between Macbeth and Lady Macbeth since Acts I and 2. It is she, not he, who must now ask 'What's to be done?'. For the moment, she is more dependent on him than he is on her. He still needs her, if only because there is nobody else in whom he can confide his secret terrors ('O, full of scorpions is my mind, dear wife!'). He becomes protective; he wants to spare her the suffering he knows would accompany the knowledge of what he is about to do ('Be innocent of the knowledge, dearest chuck,/Till thou applaud the deed . . .'). Macbeth is now the planner of dark deeds; Lady Macbeth is to play a passive role, and await news of developments from him. She will, however, regain some of her initiative in the banquet scene (Act 3, Scene 4).

ACT 3 • SCENE 3

The assassination of Banquo is carried out in darkness by
Macbeth's hirelings. Fleance escapes.

COMMENTARY

THE key word in this scene is 'mistrust'. Macbeth cannot trust his two murderers, and sends a third to make sure they do their work. The scene marks a significant change for the worse in Macbeth's position. He has failed to remove Fleance, who represents the main threat to his security and peace of mind, and at the same time has laid himself open to suspicion of involvement in Banquo's death. If Macbeth takes the prophecies of the Witches seriously, his target should be Fleance rather than Banquo. Indeed, in his soliloquy in Act 3, Scene 1, he has been deeply disturbed by the thought that 'Banquo's issue' may become kings. When the Second Murderer says that they have lost the 'Best half of our affair', he is describing Macbeth's new position quite accurately: they have allowed Fleance, the ultimate long-term threat, to flourish, and have eliminated Banquo, who, according to the Witches, cannot endanger Macbeth's throne.

ACT 3 • SCENE 4

*At the state banquet, Macbeth and Lady Macbeth welcome
their guests. Having heard about Banquo's murder in gory
detail from one of the assassins, Macbeth returns to join in the
feast, only to find Banquo's Ghost sitting in his place. He
betrays himself before his guests, who do not see the apparition,
and loses control of his feelings. Lady Macbeth strives to save
him from exposure, but fails, and the banquet ends in total
disorder. At the close of the scene, when Lady Macbeth and her
husband are alone together, she listens to his further plans with
a weary indifference.*

COMMENTARY

THE lavish state banquet should, of course, be a triumphant
celebration of Macbeth's rule, a means of winning for him the
approval of society, of making his kingship solidly respectable. Banquets
in Shakespeare are symbols of friendship and social concord, of bodily
health and health in the kingdom. The host and hostess show an almost
exaggerated anxiety to make themselves agreeable to their guests ('at first
and last,/The hearty welcome'; 'We will require her welcome'; 'they are
welcome', 'Be large in mirth'; 'good digestion wait on appetite'; 'love and
health to all'; 'I drink to the general joy of the whole table'.) But the false
appearance of pleasant sociability cannot be maintained for long. Macbeth
and his wife are not allowed to enjoy the social fruits of their crimes.
Having violated order and hospitality by murdering the king who was
their guest, they find their own kind of order violated in turn. The entry of
the First Murderer with his bloody face is symbolic of the fact that
Macbeth cannot suppress his deeds or cover them with false pretence of
order: even 'The secret'st man of blood', as Macbeth ruefully admits later,
cannot escape detection.

The infinitely more ruinous entry of Banquo's Ghost has a symbolic aspect as well as a functional one. The Witches told Banquo that his children would be kings: he now sits in Macbeth's royal seat, which his children will one day inherit. It is this apparition that destroys the occasion, and makes it end 'With most admired disorder'. For Macbeth, the banquet scene marks a turning-point because it involves his social ruin, his total loss of face in his society. It is a decisive stage in the quickening process of his isolation. In Act 3, Scene 6, we find Lennox, who has been present at the banquet, conspiring against him. Macbeth has tried to accommodate himself to his society, and failed. When, towards the end, we find him lamenting his loss of 'honour, love, obedience, troops of friends' (5, 3, 25), we inevitably think of the hasty exit of his guests in the banquet scene, and of Lady Macbeth and himself left alone on the stage amid the ruins of the feast. There is an ironic contrast between Lady Macbeth's 'You know your own degrees, sit down', at the beginning, and her 'Stand not upon the order of your going,/But go at once' at the end. The irony deepens from banquet to banquet in *Macbeth:* the first, (Act 1, Scene 7), from which Duncan retired 'In measureless content', only to be murdered in his sleep, is a travesty of hospitality; at the second, Banquo's Ghost refuses to allow Macbeth to enjoy the feasting and the hospitality he has desecrated by killing his 'chief guest'; the third is a parody of a banquet, where the Witches prepare, not nourishing foods, but revolting recipes to cause 'toil and trouble'.

In the final part of the banquet scene, after the guests have gone, we find that a distinctly new relationship has developed between Macbeth and his wife. A quotation from an account of a 1962 Stratford production in which Irene Worth played the part of Lady Macbeth throws much light on the altered nature of her role at this point: 'As she had spoken "A kind goodnight to all!" on the departure of the thanes from the disordered banquet, she had already shrunk in stature within her great robes, and her mind controlled her voice only by a great dying effort; she stood a long time without moving and then went slowly to her throne, from which she did not rise until after the scene had finished with a blackout. Her few brief words while Macbeth played out the scene were uncalculating responses when speech, of some sort, was unavoidable'. (John Russell Brown, *Shakespeare's Plays in Performance,* 1966, p 187). The strain of the events of the banquet scene, now intensified by a growing burden of guilt, has exhausted Lady Macbeth and broken her spirit, and it comes as no surprise that her next appearance is in the sleepwalking scene. The reply she makes to Macbeth's imperious question about Macduff is the strangely listless 'Did you send to him, sir?'. Her reaction to his terrible speech in reply is even more at odds with everything she has earlier seemed to represent: instead of being roused to excitement by his hints of further action, she wearily tells him that he needs sleep.

From now on, the initiative must be fully Macbeth's, since he can no longer expect help from his wife. But he no longer needs her help; he can now plan his crimes without anybody's assistance, and without being afraid that his mind will be 'full of scorpions'. It is significant that he can think of himself wading through a river of blood, and then say 'Come, we'll to sleep'. This is a measure of the distance he has travelled since the earlier scenes, when it took all of his wife's vast powers of will to persuade him to murder Duncan. The changed relationship between the two has come about, paradoxically, through Lady Macbeth's very success in making a 'man' of her husband, as she would have it (1, 7, 49). And he is soon able to outdo her in the arts of false seeming and cunning. As he learns to perfect the methods she has taught him, he keeps his precise intentions from her. After the crisis of the banquet scene, when he has faced and endured the worst that can afflict him, he is able to go on alone. Their relationship collapses. Her death will be almost an irrelevance (5, 5, 17-8).

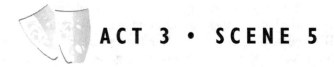

ACT 3 • SCENE 5

*Hecate, the spirit who rules over all Witches, is angry that
she has not been consulted up to now about Macbeth. She gives
orders for a meeting with him on the morrow and foretells his
downfall.*

COMMENTARY

MOST editors believe that this scene was not written by Shakespeare.
We have not been prepared for the arrival of Hecate. The Witches are
not what they were in the earlier scenes. Originally they regarded
Macbeth, like their other human contacts, as the victim of their plots; now
they seem to think of him as one of their disciples ('a wayward son'). The
last four lines of Hecate's speech, however, are worth attention, since they
refer to an important theme in the tragedy: Macbeth's reckless confidence,
which is to determine his conduct and attitudes for the rest of the play.

ACT 3 • SCENE 6

Lennox knows the extent of Macbeth's guilt. We learn that Macduff has gone to the Court of the king of England to join Malcolm.

COMMENTARY

THE main purpose of this scene is to provide a commentary on the way Macbeth's subjects feel about his reign. With obvious irony, Lennox expresses the general suspicion that Macbeth has murdered Duncan and Banquo, and sheds doubt on Macbeth's motives for killing the grooms. We are being prepared for Macbeth's move against Macduff's family, and for the role the English will play in the liberation of Scotland from Macbeth's rule. Macbeth, although a murderer, is the lawfully-crowned king of Scotland, and Shakespeare is careful to provide good reasons for a move against him. These reasons are given mainly by the anonymous lord, whose principal arguments are that Malcolm is the rightful heir to the throne, and that Macbeth's reign is a tyranny. In Act 3, Scene 4, Macbeth has announced his intention of sending for Macduff. Here we learn the result: Macduff has fled to England.

ACT 4 • SCENE 1

*The Witches prepare their spell, throwing revolting
ingredients into a boiling cauldron. Macbeth arrives, in the
hope of discovering his destiny. The Witches conjure up their
apparitions, which offer him some consolation, but which also
confirm his fears and suspicions of Macduff. Lennox brings
news that Macduff has fled to England, and Macbeth decides
on the slaughter of the fugitive's wife and children.*

COMMENTARY

THE ingredients of the Witches' cauldron are, presumably, arranged to
match Macbeth's developing wickedness. Macbeth here fulfils Hecate's
earlier prophecy (Act 3, Scene 5). He is about to be drawn on to his ruin
through over-confidence. His first greeting to the Witches is frenzied; he is
carried away by the force of his own inflated rhetoric.

The three apparitions are deceptive. The 'armed head' foretells
Macbeth's decapitation by Macduff; Macbeth, however, takes it to
represent Macduff, on whom his fears are now centred, and is thankful for
the warning the apparitions seem to convey. The Second Apparition, the
'bloody child', is Macduff, 'from his mother's womb/Untimely ripped', as we
will learn in the last act of the play. This apparition is 'More potent than
the first', because Macduff's strange birth will make him the means of
Macbeth's destruction. The advice of this apparition is cruelly misleading
to Macbeth; it urges him to remain utterly secure, since 'none of woman
born' can harm him. What Macbeth cannot know, however, is that the
speaker represents somebody not 'of woman born', and therefore the agent
of Macbeth's death. The Third Apparition is young Malcolm, coming to
Dunsinane carrying a bough. Again, Macbeth is falsely reassured by the
misleading prophecy about the moving of Birnam wood to Dunsinane.

Macbeth wants reassurance, and he is prepared to see the three
apparitions as offering this. He takes everything they say and represent

as a good omen. ('Sweet bodements! Good!'). The last part of the Witches' tableau, however, can offer little comfort. The show of eight kings, representing the eventual succession of Banquo's descendants to the throne of Scotland, is a shattering experience for Macbeth, leading him to an outburst of helpless rage. He finds some relief in his determination to murder Macduff's family. This new plan marks an obvious deterioration in Macbeth's character. The murders of Duncan and Banquo had their own terrible logic, at least from Macbeth's point of view. But the planned killing of an innocent woman and her children can achieve no practical result; it is a piece of gratuitous villainy.

ACT 4 • SCENE 2

*The location is Macduff's castle. Ross tells Lady Macduff
and her son that Macduff has fled to England. She is angry and
confused at Macduff's apparent desertion of her and her family.
A messenger comes to warn her of immediate danger. It is too
late. Macbeth's murderers arrive, kill her son, and go in pursuit
of Lady Macduff herself.*

COMMENTARY

HERE a harmless, innocent, pathetically vulnerable family group
awaits execution. The inoffensiveness of Lady Macduff is emphasised
('I have done no harm'). Many readers and spectators have found her
clever, precocious son rather difficult to take. The exchanges between
mother and son tend to detract from, rather than enhance, the pathos of
the scene as a whole.

The killing of young Macduff in full view of the audience is the most
harrowing moment of the play. At this point, sympathy for Macbeth and
all he stands for reaches its lowest ebb. It should be noted, however, that
Macbeth does not do the deed himself, and it is possible to feel that he
would not have been able to do it. The nervous anxiety of the messenger
underlines the effects of Macbeth's tyranny on his subjects: secrecy and
intrigue have become conditions of survival.

 # ACT 4 • SCENE 3

*Macduff and Malcolm are together at the English Court.
Malcolm tests Macduff's loyalty by pretending to be a reckless
libertine, totally unfitted to replace Macbeth as king. As
Macduff turns away in despair, Malcolm reveals that he is
really a virtuous young man, and now accepts Macduff's loyalty
without question. Ross comes with news of opposition to
Macbeth in Scotland and is finally forced to reveal that
Macduff's wife and family have been slain.*

COMMENTARY

THE scene falls naturally into three divisions: (a) Malcolm's testing of Macduff (*ll.* 1-139); (b) the Doctor's account of Edward the Confessor (*ll.* 140-59); (c) the news of the murders of all the members of Macduff's family and of unrest in Scotland.

The scene as a whole has attracted much unfavourable comment for its supposed lack of dramatic power, for an element of tediousness in the long exchange between Malcolm and Macduff at the beginning, and because for all its length, it does comparatively little to advance the action. But each of the three sections outlined above can be defended on a variety of grounds. From them we learn more fully than we do elsewhere the damage Macbeth has done to Scotland; the scene as a whole functions as a choric commentary in this respect. It illustrates the deviousness to which even men like Malcolm must resort in times of political tyranny, when spies are everywhere. Macduff's interview with Malcolm and its outcome help to bring matters to a head. At this point, too, the characters of both Malcolm and Macduff need development, if the two are to appear convincing and sympathetic as Macbeth's conquerors and as champions of the new order in Scotland. The scene fulfils this function.

Malcolm's elaborate testing of Macduff is best seen in conjunction with his father's fatal error of judgement in relation to both Thanes of

Cawdor. Malcolm has experienced the sad consequences of trusting even those who appear — as Macduff does — most sympathetic and helpful. He has learned early in his life that 'To show an unfelt sorrow is an office/Which the false man does easy' (2, 3, 135-6). His anxiety not to be trapped as his father was is reflected in his tortuous probing of Macduff's character and motives. Macduff's integrity is confirmed in his eyes by the latter's outburst of feeling (102-14), and by the news which Ross brings.

Another function of the scene is to establish an important set of contrasts between opposing kinds of kingship, and between opposing attitudes and reactions to similar events. One example of the latter is Macduff's response to the news of his wife's death, a response which is in marked contrast to Macbeth's reception of similar news. Malcolm is, of course, pretending to be an utterly unfit candidate for monarchy, but what he is really describing in his unflattering 'self-portrait' is Macbeth's conduct as king. And against this — we have three presentations of virtuous kingship. The first lists the 'king becoming graces', the qualities a king should have (*ll.* 91-4). The second reminds us that Duncan was 'a most sainted king' (*l.* 109). The third embodies a more palpable contrast to Macbeth's rule. Edward the Confessor is the ideal monarch. His activities are invested with religious associations ('sanctity'; 'heaven'; 'miraculous work'; 'healing benediction'; 'sundry blessings'; 'full of grace'), while Macbeth's proceedings are almost invariably characterised, both by himself and by others, in terms of images of hell, disease and damnation. Edward heals his subjects; Macbeth murders his. Edward prays; Macbeth curses, and is damned both in his own estimation and in that of others. At the Court of Edward, holy arts are practised; but in the Witches' cavern, Macbeth's place of resort, evil charms are concocted. Edward spreads benedictions whereas the air around the Witches is infected. The disease imagery used by the Doctor in this scene should be contrasted with that used by the other Doctor in Act 5, Scene I, and by Macbeth himself in Act 5, Scene 3 ('Throw physic to the dogs').

ACT 5 • SCENE 1

*In Dunsinane castle, a deranged Lady Macbeth is
sleepwalking. She relives the guilt and terror associated with
the crimes committed by her husband and herself.*

COMMENTARY

LADY Macbeth's last appearance was at the end of Act 3, Scene 4, where her tremendous effort to save appearances for Macbeth taxed her resources and resulted in the almost total collapse of her will power. At that point she had become a mere shadow of her former self, reacting passively to her dominant husband.

In this scene we find the process of Lady Macbeth's disintegration carried a step further. There was a time when she felt able to dismiss the guilty fears of her husband with contempt, since she did not share them: her mind and her imagination were free of all the haunting terrors that pursued him and destroyed his peace. Now it is her turn to be harried by guilt-ridden fancies. She was once able to reduce the supernatural and the mysterious to the level of commonplace, everyday experience ('The sleeping and the dead/Are but as pictures'). Now in this scene we find that her very reason has broken down, and that she is in the grip of terrifying, unknown fears. The sleepwalking scene, a soliloquy unheard even by its speaker, is a brilliantly successful means of revealing her subconscious acknowledgement of the forces she has so long denied. The womanly nature she has violated in a frightening display of 'manliness' now takes its revenge and demands its payment. The price she must pay is a frightful one: the loss of her reason. Macbeth has known all along that whoever dares to do more than is proper to a human being will forfeit humanity. Lady Macbeth is now learning this lesson, painfully and too late.

What is happening to Lady Macbeth in this scene illustrates the truth of D. J. Enright's remark about an essential difference between the two main characters. Lady Macbeth, he points out, 'was a sprinter in evil; her husband, slower to get off the mark, is a long-distance runner — and he continues to run though he knows that the prize is irrevocably lost'.

Lady Macbeth's disjointed talk in the sleepwalking scene has one controlling theme: guilty recollection of past deeds. She relives the circumstances of Duncan's murder ('the old man . . . so much blood in/him'). The blood she could once wash so easily from her hands will not now go away ('Here's the smell of the blood still'). The memory of the killing of Macduff's family is pathetically evoked ('The Thane of Fife had a wife: where is she now?'). These reminiscences are shot through with a tender and moving concern for her dream husband, as she imagines herself trying to strengthen and support him in his actions ('none can call our power to account . . . you mar all with this starting . . . Wash your hands, put on your nightgown . . . Banquo's buried . . . What's done/cannot be undone'). The scene ends on a note of irony. Lady Macbeth is deluded into feeling close to her husband ('come,/come, come, come, give me your hand') at the very time when their relationship has collapsed, certainly in Macbeth's eyes. We are soon to learn that she no longer occupies any place in Macbeth's world: her death will come to him as an annoying irrelevance ('She should have died hereafter').

ACT 5 • SCENE 2

Those of his own countrymen who have turned against
Macbeth are preparing for the arrival of the English forces near
Birnam wood. Reports suggest that Macbeth's support is
declining, as growing numbers desert his cause.

COMMENTARY

ALL the significant things in this scene concern Macbeth. The descriptions of his enemies gathering to overthrow him are relatively uninteresting and uninspiring. The really vivid images are reserved for him. The comment of Angus about a giant's robe hanging on a dwarfish thief, if taken too seriously as an account of Macbeth's situation, can mislead. Some commentators seem to think that here Shakespeare means us to regard Macbeth, personifying evil, as having shrunk to insignificance in the face of the advancing forces of good. This view is certainly not borne out by Macbeth's subsequent appearances; he is never dwarfish, either in a physical or in a moral sense. If he were, the ending of the play would be simply a bore, which it certainly is not. Menteith's comment is much nearer the mark:

> Who then shall blame
> His pestered senses to recoil and start,
> When all that is within him does condemn
> Itself for being there?
>
> (*ll*. 22-5)

At this point, the real interest is not in the outward action, what happens to Macbeth or to his opponents in battle, but in what is going on in his mind. This is where the focus of attention is increasingly directed. The most memorable things in the final scenes are the soliloquies in which he records his world-weariness and radical disillusionment, the emptiness of a life without significance or hope.

ACT 5 • SCENE 3

*Macbeth is at bay in Dunsinane castle. He violently
rebukes all bringers of bad news as cowards. He derives no
consolation from the Doctor's unhelpful account of Lady
Macbeth's illness, and looks to him for a remedy to cure the
maladies afflicting the country.*

COMMENTARY

IN the previous scene, Menteith has given a clue to Macbeth's behaviour.
In this one, Macbeth is showing signs of strain; his 'pestered senses' are
his overwrought nerves, which 'recoil' or give way as further troubles
come. His behaviour now is certainly volatile. He is given to sudden
changes of mood. His first speech is marked by a false sense of security: he
still trusts the 'spirits that know/All mortal consequence'. He momentarily
loses control at the news of the approach of the English army, treating the
unfortunate messenger with cruel contempt. Then he lapses suddenly into
a pitiful, despairing, extremely moving reflection on his desolate life, a life
which he finds increasingly intolerable. This mood is succeeded by one of
determination to face all the odds bravely ('I'll fight, till from my bones my
flesh be hacked'). Again, he becomes reflective and philosophical, as he
broods on the power of medicine to eradicate the troubles of the brain, and
extends his meditation to developing an analogy between the troubles of
the human body and those of the Commonwealth. At the end, he resumes
his blustering, dare-devil attitude ('I will not be afraid of death and bane').

ACT 5 • SCENE 4

Malcolm orders the assembled soldiers to cut boughs from Birnam wood in order to mislead Macbeth regarding their numbers. They make their way towards Macbeth's stronghold.

COMMENTARY

THE arrangements ordered by Malcolm in this scene ('Let every soldier hew him down a bough') prepare us for the unfortunate working-out of one prophecy for Macbeth. We now know that Birnam wood is about to 'move' to Dunsinane, and that the confidence Macbeth has just expressed at the end of Act 5, Scene 3, is not soundly based. If he knew the whole truth he would have every reason to be afraid of 'death and bane'.

ACT 5 • SCENE 5

Macbeth prepares to offer stiff resistance to his enemy; just then he hears of his wife's death. His response is to comment on the futility of human life and its transitory nature. A messenger brings news that Birnam wood is moving towards Dunsinane. Macbeth, although he now senses that his cause is lost, is determined to die fighting.

COMMENTARY

THE focal point of the scene is Macbeth's great soliloquy (*ll.* 17-28), which is his response to the news of Lady Macbeth's death. Macbeth's existence has been drained of all significance; he sees one day creeping after another in the same trivial ('petty') way, until life ends. In lines 22-3 we have the image of poor, foolish, deluded human beings having only enough light to find their way to the darkness of death. The idea of death as 'dusty' derives from the image 'dust to dust'. Life is like a candle-flame, extinguished all too quickly. It is a 'walking shadow'; here Shakespeare wants us to picture the doomed human fools finding their way to their dusty deaths with the aid of candles, and casting shadows as they walk along. The miserable chronicle of all those yesterdays is a reminder of the futility of human effort. 'Shadow' refers back to the candle and forward to the 'poor player', since the acting he does is only a shadow of reality. The human actor is 'poor' because he is to be pitied: he is soon to be silenced by death; he is also poor because he plays his part without proper dignity, straining for effect ('struts and frets'). In lines 26-8 life is no longer seen in terms of the human action represented by fools walking to death or the poor actor strutting on the stage. It becomes even more unreal: it is merely a meaningless story told by an idiot speaker.

The messenger who interrupts Macbeth's meditation is another speaker, a frightened man, looking almost idiotic, who has to tell *his* strange, incomprehensible story, the story of a wood that moves.

Macbeth's most famous speech ends with a view of man as a pawn or puppet 'activated by an uncomprehending and mad creator', as one critic describes it. Another critic sees the speech as a reflection of 'the nothingness that life becomes to him before it is taken from him'. It should be noted that Shakespeare makes much use of biblical allusion throughout. The candle and shadow images are found in the Book of Job (18:6 and 8:9) and the Psalms (18:28 and 39:7), while the metaphor of life as a tale is found in Psalm 99: 'We bring our years to an end as a tale that is told'.

The speech as a whole, but particularly the player-image, is a point of convergence for several lines of imagery developed throughout the play: the interlocked images of desire and act, appearance and reality, clothes that fit another and cannot be borrowed, daggers breeched with gore and painted faces — all have a relation to stage-business. In an earlier speech, Lady Macbeth reminded her husband that the sleeping and the dead were no more real than pictures (2, 2, 54-5). Macbeth has now come to regard everything, even life itself, as unreal. He has, for the moment, cut himself adrift from all that has bound him to solid reality, and entered a world of illusions.

The full power of the speech can be realised only in performance. For some of the lines to take on their full meaning, it is necessary for them to be spoken on the stage, or at least for the reader to visualise their being spoken by Macbeth. As he speaks the fourth line for example, ('Creeps in this petty pace') and the ninth ('That struts and frets his hour upon the stage'), he is pacing the stage, enacting his meaning. Again, gesture and movement lend an added significance to lines 22-3. 'And all our yesterdays' is accompanied by a sweeping movement of the hand, which points limply to the ground at 'dusty death'.

The play does not end on the despairing note sounded at the end of this soliloquy. In his final moments, Macbeth emerges from his vision of a totally meaningless world. He again faces life in a way which suggests his recognition that some things at least retain significance for him. His display of courage and determination, his refusal to yield to a future of mockery and humiliation — these are not meaningless gestures.

ACT 5 • SCENES 6 AND 7

The battle begins outside the castle, Macbeth's last
stronghold. Macbeth emerges, and kills young Siward. Macduff
seeks out Macbeth, whose castle at last falls to his enemies.

COMMENTARY

THE 'leafy screens' of Scene 6 fulfil the prophecy made by the Third
Apparition in Act 4, Scene I. They are also symbols of the new kind of
life that is in store for Scotland following Macbeth's fall.

The opening of Scene 7 shows Macbeth possessed by a rugged
determination to face a situation that he now knows is desperate. His
enemies have closed in on him, and escape is impossible: hence his image
of himself as a bear tied to a stake, at the mercy of savage dogs. However,
he still clutches at the Witches' promise that only a man not born of
woman can kill him.

There are three other very brief episodes in this scene. Young Siward
hopes to achieve a heroic reputation by killing Macbeth, but in this he
fails. Macbeth's success here renews his confidence in his safety ('Thou
wast born of woman'). Macduff stresses his strong personal motives for
confronting Macbeth: the ghosts of his wife and children will always haunt
him if he fails to avenge them personally. The third episode, featuring the
arrival of Malcolm and Old Siward, deals with the larger political theme.
The final collapse of Macbeth's cause is suggested in Malcolm's ambiguous
'We have met with foes/That strike beside us'; this may mean either that
Macbeth's soldiers have joined his enemies or that they are deliberately
not fighting very hard.

ACT 5 • SCENE 8

Macbeth and Macduff face each other. Macbeth boasts that
he is invulnerable to any man born of woman, but Macduff
shatters his confidence by revealing the strange circumstances
surrounding his own birth. Macbeth dies fighting fiercely for
the life he has not long before described as meaningless.

COMMENTARY

THERE is a suggestion at the beginning of the scene that Macbeth has
been contemplating suicide as an alternative to defeat and surrender,
only to reject the idea decisively in favour of killing more enemies. His
response to Macduff has two elements: guilt at the thought of the suffering
he has already inflicted on Macduff, and misplaced confidence in his
(Macbeth's) ability to overcome him. When this confidence is shattered by
Macduff's revelation of the strange manner of his birth, Macbeth's natural
instinct is to run away ('I'll not fight with thee'). Macduff's taunting cry of
'coward' causes him to adopt his characteristic stance, and to die fighting,
rather than face the prospect of humiliation.

ACT 5 • SCENE 9

The victors congratulate themselves on their success, and Macduff enters with Macbeth's head. Malcolm, the new king, pledges that he will restore order and harmony to Scotland, and repeats the rumour that Lady Macbeth has died by her own hand.

COMMENTARY

IT is difficult to be enthusiastic about this final scene. The play ends on a falling note. After the tempestuous earlier scenes involving Macbeth, the congratulations and rejoicings of his enemies are a tame affair. Good has triumphed and the forces of evil have been overcome; but, in the process, all that gave the play its life and excitement has been banished. Set against Macbeth's terrible and heart-rending utterances during his final hours, the sentiments expressed by his conquerors seem utterly pallid and uninspiring.

The Characters

MACBETH

EVERY serious account of Macbeth's character must involve three elements. The first element is Macbeth's status as tragic hero. The central figure in any tragedy must command and retain the earnest good will of the audience. He must be the kind of character who can compel an audience not merely to follow his fortunes with intense interest, but to become emotionally involved with him as well.

The second essential element in any discussion of Macbeth is his role as villain-hero: he is a man whose career throughout the play is marked by a steady moral decline. This aspect is memorably charted by Helen Gardner, who describes Macbeth's tragedy as a path to damnation, beginning at one extreme and ending at another: 'From a brave and loyal general, to a treacherous murderer, to a hirer of assassins, to an employer of spies, to a butcher, to a coward, to a thing with no feeling for anything but itself, to a monster and a hell-hound'.

The third element that must be considered is how tragic hero and villain-hero are reconciled in the play. How, in other words, does Shakespeare maintain for Macbeth the full stature of a tragic hero in the face of the horrific deeds he plans and perpetrates?

A BRAVE AND LOYAL GENERAL

It is instructive to examine the various ways in which Shakespeare works to enlist and maintain our sympathy for his deeply-flawed central figure. If we are to regard Macbeth's fall as a genuinely tragic event, he must be seen as a man of worth and significance to begin with, since the downfall of a worthless, insignificant character would not be tragic. *Macbeth* answers in many ways to the classical concept of *hubris;* the great man overreaches his ambitions and must inevitably collapse. In the early scenes, Shakespeare establishes Macbeth as a valued member of his society, the saviour of his country, the favourite of his king. His nobility, bravery and soldiership are stressed by several speakers. He is 'brave Macbeth', 'noble Macbeth', 'Bellona's bridegroom'. It is true, however, that even in these early accounts of Macbeth's heroism in battle, a disturbing note is sounded. There is an air of barbaric ferocity about the descriptions of his achievements on the battlefield. The Macbeth we are invited to admire carries a sword that smokes with bloody execution: he rips his enemy open, and hacks his way through the massed ranks of the opposing armies. This, however, is not allowed to count against Macbeth. Indeed, soon after, we are given a convincing testimonial to the fundamental goodness of his character by an expert witness, his wife. In her very first comment on him, she regrets that his goodness will make it extremely difficult for him to fulfil his ambition by unlawful means: he lacks the ruthless, evil touch she associates with successful men.

A RELUCTANT CRIMINAL

But Macbeth, for all his fundamental virtue, murders Duncan. This act, however, is surrounded by contradictory features. His behaviour before the murder, and his reaction to it, suggest very strongly that he is not well adapted to the role of murderer. He is a reluctant criminal, hesitating beforehand, making a powerful case against what he is about to do, and then approaching the deed itself with horror. No sooner has he killed Duncan than he is wishing his victim alive again. We should condemn Macbeth, and condemnation is certainly part of our response to his murder of his guest and kinsman. But as things are presented by Shakespeare, pity for the murderer tends to overwhelm pity for the victim. There is first of all the feeling that he has been morally blackmailed by his wife into perpetrating the crime. It is important to observe that he is not shown killing Duncan, nor do we see or hear anything of the king's final moments. What we are given instead is Macbeth's appalled response to what he has done: his self-condemnation, his self-disgust, his terrified consciousness that he could not pray and that he will sleep no more. We are made to share, and to sympathise with, his realisation that the Duncan who now sleeps in the peace of death is happier than he himself is. Macbeth is seen as the pitiful victim of a crime he was unwilling to commit in the first place, a victim who knows that he is doomed to live out his life in the shadow of that crime. He has lost his inward peace, and his life has been deprived of much of its meaning and interest. In the aftermath of the murder, then, one's attention is strongly focused on Macbeth's sufferings and his victim tends to be largely forgotten.

'A MONSTER AND A HELL-HOUND'

As the play progresses, Macbeth's deeds become more revolting to our feelings and to our moral sense. This is mainly because, unlike Duncan's murder, they are undertaken willingly and with a show of ghoulish enthusiasm. It thus follows that it becomes increasingly difficult for Shakespeare to retain our sympathy for his villain-hero. The carefully planned murder of Banquo must inevitably alienate the sympathy of any audience from Macbeth. Banquo, after all, has been allowed by Shakespeare to make a more profound appeal to imaginations and feelings than Duncan has, and in this case Macbeth lacks the excuse that the deed was thrust upon him by somebody else.

The events leading up to Banquo's murder reveal a new and less attractive side to Macbeth. He is now seen as a cunning, calculating and deceitful man; he suffers a sharp moral decline. We see no evidence now of the guilt-haunted, tormented, reluctant criminal who carried out Duncan's murder. Even here, however, Shakespeare does not totally deprive Macbeth of our pity and understanding. He preserves him from direct contact with the murder of Banquo, which is performed by hired assassins. The pity we feel for Banquo is soon engulfed in the overcharged emotion of the banquet scene, where the focus is entirely on Macbeth's tortured response to the ghost.

With the murder of Lady Macduff and her children, a new sense of Macbeth's moral decline forces itself upon us. The presentation of these murders is much more direct and immediate than was the case with those of Duncan and Banquo. The latest murders are enacted in broad daylight and in full view of the audience, while the sympathetic portrayal of Lady Macduff just before she is murdered adds to the outrage which the deed provokes. At this point, our sympathy with Macbeth's victims and enemies is at its peak. And after this, it is inevitable that we should side emotionally as well as intellectually with the forces preparing for his overthrow. It is characteristic of Shakespeare's presentation that the murder of Lady Macduff and her children is soon followed by the sleepwalking scene, which marks the utter breakdown of the relationship between Macbeth and Lady Macbeth. Macbeth's third major crime is thus followed by the mental and emotional collapse of his 'partner of greatness'.

SHARING 'THE ACHE OF THE MIND DISEASED'

In Act 5, when Macbeth's moral decline has been unmistakably established, and when his fall from prosperity is inevitable, the audience again becomes deeply involved emotionally with his fortunes. Shakespeare reserves some of the finest dramatic verse of his maturity to convey Macbeth's sense of utter loss, his nostalgia for an irrecoverable and irredeemable past, his sense of a hopeless and meaningless present and future. In his account of Sir Laurence Olivier's portrayal of Macbeth, the theatre critic Richard David recalls how that great actor could maintain the sympathy of the audience for Macbeth's nightmare vision. Olivier's Macbeth, as David remembers him, was 'a man possessed, but no petty devil. Even when the audience had long changed sides, and stood with the heaven-blest justicers from England, it could still be drawn to feel and to share the ache of the mind diseased, the rooted sorrow'.

The grandeur and pathos of Macbeth's great speeches in Act 5 cast a powerful spell, difficult to resist even in the face of all we know and condemn in the speaker. The forces of virtue assembling to overthrow him seem petty and insignificant when placed against his sensitivity to suffering and despair. The doomed, damned villain comes to accept himself as he is, and dies a warrior's death.

Thus, Shakespeare's presentation of Macbeth is such that the reader or spectator, while fully sensitive to the horror of his actions and his moral decline, must nevertheless feel the force of his latent nobility, together with a sense of outrage at the tragic waste of so much goodness. Every interpretation of the final scenes must take account of the dual nature of the tragic hero. On the one hand, there is the fiercely defiant Macbeth facing his enemies like a trapped animal. On the other, there is the tormented soul overwhelmed by self-hatred and despair, the suffering victim of his own deeds. We can do justice to the complexity of the characterisation only if we give due emphasis to the conscience-stricken murderer of Duncan, the honoured general, the loving husband, the cunning contriver of Banquo's death, the imaginative interpreter of the movements of his own mind, the enigma of good and evil, strength and weakness.

MACBETH — A FULLY RESPONSIBLE AGENT?

Discussion of Macbeth's activities tends to concentrate on two issues, responsibility and motivation. Many accounts of his character are composed in terms of unqualified moral condemnation. It should be borne · in mind that if we are to condemn him roundly in this way, we must hold him morally responsible for his actions, and assume that he is an entirely free agent acting with full deliberation, aware at all stages of the meaning and consequences of his conduct. But the question must be asked: do these considerations apply to his murder of Duncan? Those who say that they do can point to the remarkable soliloquy ('If it were done, when 'tis done' 1, 7, 1-28), in which he analyses in close and convincing detail what the murder of Duncan must mean for him morally and spiritually. He is fully aware that his projected deed will be a violation of the moral and social order, as well as of the laws of hospitality, friendship and kinship. But like other tragic heroes, Macbeth is, to a large extent, the victim of tragic blindness. He cannot foresee that the apparent success attending the first murder will lead to further killings and to progressive degradation.

Again, when we are considering Macbeth's responsibility for the murder of Duncan, we must take account of Lady Macbeth's part in disturbing his moral balance. She uses her massive powers of will and character to confuse and browbeat him. He is prepared to take a stand on moral grounds against the murder ('We will proceed no further in this business' 1, 7, 31). She bullies him into regarding the issue as a test of his manliness and of his love for her. He loses the argument. She narrows the discussion to a single point — not whether the murder is right or wrong, but whether or not they will get away with it. Once she has destroyed his moral defences, the rest is easy, and her dubious plan for the murder convinces him. The very fact that he so readily accepts her scheme, and makes an enthusiastic comment on it, suggests that Macbeth is far from being a fully responsible agent at this vital point.

VAULTING AMBITION?

What of Macbeth's motivation? It is common for critics to identify ambition and lust for power as the twin forces inspiring him to launch his murderous career. In support of this they can cite his reference to 'Vaulting ambition' as his spur to action. The critic A. C. Bradley argued eloquently that 'Macbeth's passion for power and his instinct for self-assertion and self-advancement are such that no inward misery can persuade him to relinquish the fruits of his crime'. The truth is, however, that no simple, straightforward account of Macbeth's motivation is satisfactory. One major problem for anybody trying to probe his motives, particularly for Duncan's murder, is that his actions appear to run counter to his deepest feelings, instincts and mental habits. It is often suggested that Shakespeare failed to provide adequate and convincing motives for Macbeth's crimes, particularly his killing of Duncan. He could, for example, have made Duncan a bad king and an unsympathetic individual, and given Macbeth some justified grievances. Instead, Duncan appears virtuous and good-natured, and Macbeth, far from having grievances against him, owes a great deal to his kindness and generosity.

For an initial motive, we are forced back to ambition and a lust for power. But even this motive is not presented very convincingly. All that Lady Macbeth can say about him in this regard is that he is 'not without ambition'; he himself mentions 'Vaulting ambition' as his spur to action. But when all is said and done, Macbeth's motives and acts defy logical analysis. His first murder horrifies him before, during and after its commission. He approaches it like a maniac in a trance. As we watch him, we are hardly convinced that he is killing Duncan mainly to satisfy ambition. He acts in a state of bewilderment and desperation, seeking relief from the taunts of his wife and from the torments of his excited imagination.

What are we to think of Macbeth's motives for killing Banquo? An answer to this question may be sought in his soliloquy on the subject ('To be thus is nothing . . .' 3, 1, 48-72). Here Macbeth suggests that Banquo may pose a threat to his security, and that he himself has risked eternal damnation by murdering Duncan for the sake of Banquo's heirs. But has Macbeth any *practical* reason for killing Banquo? A. C. Bradley, arguing that he has, offers an interesting suggestion, based on an interpretation of the following lines, an interpretation with which not everybody will agree:

> And put a barren sceptre in my gripe,
> Thence to be wrenched with an unlineal hand,
> No son of mine succeeding
>
> 3, 1, 62-4.

Most critics assume that here Macbeth is thinking of some far-off day when power will fall from him to Banquo's descendants. Bradley, however, asserts that it is not some distant loss of power that Macbeth fears, but a sudden and secret attack on him by Banquo. It seems at least as likely that Macbeth is thinking of an 'unlineal hand' taking his sceptre after he dies a natural death.

'I HAVE SUPPED FULL OF HORRORS'

The truest explanation of Macbeth's growing desire to kill must be sought, not in any practical benefit he thinks will accrue to him through successive murders, but in the very depths of his nature. It is possible that after Duncan's death he kills again and again because he has been so brutalised by his first crime that his humane impulses have withered and died. There is an even more disturbing explanation of his murderous career. The memory of his first crime is so intolerable that he is driven to erase it by plunging into further crime. Again, he is convinced that his first crime has left him beyond hope of redemption, and that further crimes can make his position no worse than it already is: 'I am in blood/ Stepped in so far that, should I wade no more,/Returning were as tedious as go o'er' (3, 4, 136-8). In the end, motivation becomes almost irrelevant. The play is best regarded, not as an exploration of a man's motives, but of his self-destructive urge, of his capacity to perform deeds which seem contrary to his nature.

IN EXILE FROM THE DAYLIGHT WORLD

A central feature of Macbeth's career throughout the play is his progressive movement from centrality to isolation. This pattern is part of an essential process in every tragedy: the hero must confront his destiny alone. Macbeth begins his career as the most admired and valued figure of his society, and ends it in total estrangement and alienation from his people. The shape of his career is a familiar one. Having caused havoc in society and broken the laws of God and man, he must be isolated and destroyed, so that natural and social order may be restored.

The opening scenes focus attention on Macbeth as the heroic object of everybody's attention — an attention well deserved, since he is the saviour of his country. The officer's account of his exploits in Act I, Scene 2, and the king's lavish praises in Act I, Scene 4, serve to establish his heroic stature and his unique status in society before his fall. But the images used in these places to convey Macbeth's prowess as a warrior have a disturbing quality. There is a frightening savagery in some of the more memorable ones: the sword smoking with the hot blood of enemies, Macbeth ripping one of them open, and carving his way through multitudes of others. Macbeth is a man apart, not merely in his valour but in his capacity for destruction.

Before Duncan's murder we find Macbeth and Lady Macbeth taking the first decisive steps which will isolate them from the processes of normal living and break the bonds which bind them to human nature and society. With deliberate formality ('Come, you spirits . . .' Act 1, Scene 5) Lady Macbeth dedicates herself to superhuman evil powers, and Macbeth makes a similar dedication (Act 2, Scene 1). His separation from God is implied in his terrified question 'But wherefore could not I pronounce "Amen"?' (2, 2, 32).

'WHY DO YOU KEEP ALONE, ... ?

Duncan's murder hastens the process of Macbeth's isolation. Malcolm and Donalbain flee from him and Banquo suspects him. Macduff, even at an early stage, has doubts about him, and will not attend his coronation. Even before Banquo's murder and the social *débâcle* of the banquet scene, we have a glimpse of Macbeth estranged from his natural companions: 'Why do you keep alone,/Of sorriest fancies your companions making, . . .? (3, 2, 8-9).

The banquet scene (Act 3, Scene 4) marks a decisive stage in Macbeth's alienation from his subjects. His gradual estrangement even from Lady Macbeth is suggested in his failure to let her share in his plan to murder Banquo and Fleance. After her supreme effort in the banquet scene, she dwindles from being his 'dearest partner of greatness' to a passive, listless, weary listener. The last time we see him alone with her, at the end of Act 3, Scene 4, the collapse of their relationship is pathetically apparent; this is further underlined in his indifferent response to her death. The final movement of the banquet scene has compelling visual images of Macbeth's separation from his subjects, who leave his feast in hasty disorder. This is not the only abandonment. In the same scene we learn that Fleance has escaped, that Macduff refuses to come to Court at Macbeth's strict command, and that the latter can depend so little on the loyalty of his followers that he must keep a paid servant in all their houses.

'HONOUR, LOVE, OBEDIENCE, . . . I MUST NOT LOOK TO HAVE'

The final movement of the play opens with growing opposition to Macbeth's rule, and news of intrigue and conspiracy against him. In Act 5, his isolation is made explicit in reiterated images of abandonment and loneliness. He articulates it in some of the greatest poetry of the play. He regrets the loss of honour, love, obedience and a multitude of friends. Even the Doctor would desert him if he could. We are reminded often that many of his soldiers have gone over to the enemy.

There is an altogether appropriate image of his final isolation in his defiant cry: 'They have tied me to a stake; I cannot fly,/But bear-like I must fight the course' (5, 7, 1-2). In a 1962 production, Eric Porter played Macbeth and, as J. R. Brown reports, 'his death was that of a tired, angry, disarmed fighter: to make this clear he was killed on stage after he had been encircled by the entire army and had lost all his weapons'. This is not quite what Shakespeare gives us, but it vividly conveys how absolute is Macbeth's isolation at the end. The transformation from admired leader to hunted enemy is complete. The pattern of Macbeth's isolation has involved him in much more than a progressive physical and moral detachment from other human beings. He has been in exile from the world of daylight, familiar with Witches and with apparitions unseen by anybody else, making discoveries about his predicament which he could never share with others who have not dared to sound the depths of evil that he has.

LADY MACBETH

SHAKESPEARE created the character of Lady Macbeth from a few suggestions in Holinshed's *Chronicles,* the book he mainly used as the source of his play. Holinshed records that Macbeth's wife urged her husband to kill the king because she was 'very ambitious, burning in unquenchable desire to bear the name of a queen'. In Shakespeare's play, ambition is certainly a major key to her character, motives and actions. Shakespeare's presentation of Lady Macbeth is remarkable for its concentration on a few basic qualities. He endows her with courage, determination and will-power, as well as a remarkable ability to focus all her resources of mind and heart on the matter in hand. These moral qualities, which she turns to immoral ends, are much more impressive than her intellectual power. She combines a highly-developed will with a limited mental and imaginative range. Like the aunt in Saki's story *The Lumber-Room,* she is a woman of few ideas, with immense powers of concentration.

THE COURAGE OF FANTASY

The contrast between husband and wife in terms of mental and imaginative range is easily illustrated from Act I, Scene 7; this scene marks a significant stage in Macbeth's moral collapse. Up to the moment of Lady Macbeth's entry at line 28, Macbeth has been arguing himself sensibly and logically out of the murder of Duncan. Her function in this scene is mainly to turn logic on its head in an effort to convince her husband that he must kill Duncan. Her contribution lowers the intellectual tone of the scene. Her arguments are a combination of emotion, irrationality, moral blackmail (if he doesn't kill Duncan he can't really love her) and question-begging (he must kill in order to prove himself a man). The plan she devises to divert suspicion from Macbeth and herself is far from impressive, and reflects little credit on her powers of invention. She suggests that suspicion will inevitably fall on Duncan's chamberlains if Macbeth leaves their gory daggers on their pillows — as if, in the circumstances, they would be anxious to make a public declaration of their guilt. Admittedly, Macbeth enthusiastically accepts the 'plan', but this only shows her temporary dominance over his will and intellect. Her absurd arguments and suggestions are enough to bully and baffle him into acting against his better instincts.

Up to and including the banquet scene, Lady Macbeth gives some impressive displays of will-power, resourcefulness and self-control. She saves Macbeth from collapse and possible exposure after Duncan's murder. She has to attend to vital and basic practical details which in his disordered emotional state, her husband ignores. Without her prompting he could never have murdered Duncan, but without her decisive intervention, his helplessness after the murder would almost certainly have led to his discovery. Lady Macbeth's final, supreme effort is made in the banquet scene. Her performance here on her husband's behalf is magnificent. Having played a subordinate role to him in the events leading up to Banquo's murder, she now responds with all the resources of her will to the stress of crisis. She asserts her dominance over him for the last time as she rallies and rebukes him; this supreme effort, however, marks the end of her active role.

THE SEASON OF REMORSE

After the tumult of the banquet scene Lady Macbeth appears physically and emotionally drained. When she and Macbeth are alone together, she is a pathetic shadow of her earlier self. She can muster only a few words in reply to his questions, culminating in a heartfelt plea for rest.

The most merciless and pitiless of all Shakespeare's female characters now evokes pity for herself. This pity is intensified in the sleepwalking scene. One of the most moving revelations in the play is that here her tenderness towards her husband, and her concern for him ('give me your hand') survive even the collapse of their relationship. Her tragedy lies in the fact that the human nature she has so ruthlessly denied and suppressed finally avenges itself on her. She cannot bear the weight of her guilt. It is one of the most compelling ironies of the play that it is she, not Macbeth, who falls victim to the terrible visions and guilt-ridden fantasies she has warned him not to entertain. ('These deeds must not be thought/ After these ways: so, it will make us mad' 2, 2, 34-5).

A 'FIEND-LIKE QUEEN'

At the end, Malcolm pronounces Lady Macbeth's epitaph: she is the 'fiend-like queen'. This kind of comment is easy to dismiss as the conventionally abusive propaganda of an enemy, but there may well be more to it than that. There is convincing evidence that Shakespeare's early audiences would have regarded Lady Macbeth as a woman possessed by devils. In this regard, the key speech is the one beginning 'Come, you spirits,/That tend on mortal thoughts, . . .' (1, 5, 39-53). Her invocation of these spirits and of the 'murdering ministers' is one of the formal stages of demonic possession. She is inviting the powers of evil to take possession of her, body and soul. The 'sightless substances' she mentions in the same speech are spirits that wait for evidence of wicked thoughts that will facilitate their passage through the human will into the body. The wicked thoughts in this case are thoughts of murder.

The notion that Lady Macbeth is literally possessed by demons helps to account for the unnatural darkness surrounding the castle, the Porter's talk of the castle entrance as hell-gate, the unnatural portents on the night of the murder, as well as the horrors of the sleepwalking scene, where the Doctor realises that she needs the services of a priest more than those of a physician. Her self-dedication to evil, exemplified in the invocation of the spirits, is quite deliberate, in a way that Macbeth's is not. He, as Hecate points out, is only a 'wayward son' of evil. She asks in the most formal way that whatever natural tendencies she may have towards goodness and compassion may be eliminated. The speech involves a total rejection of her human instincts and her femininity. In her acceptance of evil as good, she takes her place with the Witches and Hecate, the forces of preternatural wickedness.

BANQUO

APART from Macbeth and Lady Macbeth, Banquo is the most fully developed of the characters. One of his most important functions in the early scenes is to act as a foil to Macbeth. Banquo's innocence and fundamental goodness are contrasted with Macbeth's guilt at various points. There is no evidence in the first two Acts that Banquo is anything but honourable and high-minded. His response to the Witches is clearly in marked contrast to Macbeth's. When he and Macbeth confront them (Act 1, Scene 3), Banquo shows neither the fear nor the agitation of his partner. Nor does he share Macbeth's intense interest in what the Witches have to say. Indeed, he is surprised at Macbeth's fearful response, and wonders at his obvious preoccupation with what he has been told. When Banquo hears the predictions concerning himself he does not respond: unlike Macbeth, he does not ask to hear more. His judgement of the significance of the Witches is sounder than Macbeth's. When part of their prediction is quickly verified with the news that Macbeth is the new Thane of Cawdor, he senses that the Witches have derived their prophetic powers from evil sources.

A MAN OF INTEGRITY

Banquo's freedom from guilt and his good nature are stressed in the scene he shares with Duncan and Macbeth (Act 1, Scene 4). He appears utterly free from envy or self-interest. At this point, Macbeth has been honoured by the king with Cawdor's title. Banquo, whom Duncan acknowledges as having deserved no less than Macbeth, gets no reward for his services, but makes no complaint. Indeed, the scene closes with Duncan's pleased recognition of Banquo's lavish praises of Macbeth. Two scenes later, we are given a further pleasing impression of Banquo's nature. His sensitive description of the attractions of Macbeth's castle for the 'temple-haunting martlet' is most appealing, the index of a mind untroubled by Macbeth's dark thoughts, at peace with itself and in harmony with its surroundings.

The opening of Act 2 marks a change in Banquo's mood, perhaps in his attitudes, although the matter is not absolutely clear. He is troubled not merely by the gloom of the night, but by the bad dreams he has been having. It is, however, significant that he has not given way to temptation as Macbeth has done. Instead he prays for the strength to overcome it: the 'Merciful Powers' he calls upon are the heavenly agents who are supposed to combat the activities of evil spirits. We soon learn the cause of Banquo's anxiety: he has, he tells Macbeth, dreamt of 'the three Weird Sisters', and is impressed by the fact that they have told Macbeth the truth. When Macbeth makes what may well be a treasonable suggestion ('If you shall cleave to my consent . . . It shall make honour for you'), Banquo's reply seems to confirm his integrity. He will not entertain any proposal that will compromise his allegiance or his honour.

In the scene following Duncan's murder (Act 2, Scene 3), Banquo again earns respect for his principled stand and his courageous statement of his integrity. He puts Lady Macbeth down with a sharp rejoinder ('Too cruel anywhere') to her complaint that Duncan has been murdered in *her* house. Towards the end of the scene he asserts his own high-minded attitude to all that has happened, and dissociates himself from the 'treasonous malice' involved in Duncan's murder. He goes further. He is ready to join those who would investigate the crime, and to fight for what he sees as right.

THE ENIGMATIC BANQUO

After Act 2, Scene 3, we are suddenly confronted with doubts about Banquo's character and motives. We know from his soliloquy at the beginning of Act 3 that he is convinced of Macbeth's guilt ('Thou play'dst most foully for't') but he has, in spite of his earlier declarations, taken no action against Macbeth. Far from it. He seems to have accepted Macbeth's kingship without undue scruple, and declares himself bound to his king 'with a most indissoluble tie'. Banquo acts as Macbeth's advisor on affairs of State. We hear nothing now of Banquo's high principles. Instead, his final soliloquy suggests that he has dynastic ambitions. He thinks of the Witches as oracles who may yet do as much for him as they have done for

Macbeth ('And set me up in hope?'). How Banquo may think these hopes are to be realised is another matter. There are those who suggest that, having decided to collaborate with Macbeth, he is hoping that his son may profit from Macbeth's crime. If we take the least favourable view of the evidence in Act 3, Scene 1, we may feel that Banquo's nature has been tainted, if not corrupted, by ambition, that he has come to terms with evil, and that only his death saves him from a dishonourable end. If this interpretation is correct, then his dramatic progress is parallel to Macbeth's, with the downward curve suddenly cut short at Act 3, Scene 3. His career would then illustrate the truth of Malcolm's later assertion that 'A good and virtuous nature may recoil/In an imperial charge' (4, 3, 19-20).

 **DUNCAN**

D UNCAN appears only in three scenes up to the scene in which he is murdered. Shakespeare does comparatively little to stamp the king with any striking individual features. He belongs to an older generation than that of Macbeth and Lady Macbeth: Lady Macbeth, long after his death, wonders that so old a man could have had 'so much blood in/him'. Old he may be, but he need not be played or pictured as a dotard. His lively concern about his rebel enemy ('Is execution done on Cawdor?') and his conduct of affairs of State and of ceremonial suggest an alert, active mind.

Duncan is presented, however, less as a complete human being than as an ideal of kingship. He is, on all the evidence we have, a model king. He is remembered nostalgically by Macduff as 'a most sainted king'. The most convincing tributes to his goodness as a man and his qualities as a monarch come from Macbeth, who mentions his humility and his fair-mindedness in the performance of his duties (he has 'borne his faculties so meek' and has been 'So clear in his great office'). His kindness and generosity are heavily underlined as his death approaches. He lavishes honours and praises on Macbeth and Banquo and promises more; he greets his hostess with an expensive gift. He is, in all of this, the victim of the profoundest irony.

Duncan's death is marked by acute disturbances in nature and a genuine grief on the part of all good men. Even Macbeth cannot avoid expressing the true significance of the terrible event:

> renown and grace is dead,
> The wine of life is drawn, and the mere lees
> Is left this vault to brag of
>
> 2, 3, 93-5.

MACDUFF

THERE are three main movements in the play, each one featuring Macbeth in fatal conflict with another character. The first movement ends with the murder of Duncan, the second with that of Banquo, and the third, involving Macbeth and Macduff as mighty opposites, ends with Macbeth's death at the hands of the man he has so cruelly wronged.

The character of Macduff, like Duncan, is not developed in any great detail by Shakespeare. There is no subtlety in the presentation of his role. He is the man of principle, loyal to his king and to his country. He appears to harbour shrewd doubts about Macbeth from the time of Duncan's death. His attitude to his new king is suggested in his brief exchange with Ross at the end of Act 2. Ross is preparing to go to Scone to attend Macbeth's coronation. Macduff will not attend ('No, cousin, I'll to Fife'), and furthermore, he hints at his doubts and anxieties about what Macbeth's reign may mean for Scotland ('adieu!/Lest our old robes sit easier than our new!').

Macduff does not become a significant character until the beginning of Act 4 when the Witches warn Macbeth against him, and when he flees to England to seek help for the forces opposed to Macbeth. He is presented from then on as a major focus of opposition to Macbeth's rule. He plays the dominant role in the longest scene in the play (Act 4, Scene 3). Here he emerges as a patriot, determined to right his country's wrongs, loyal to Malcolm and to the memory of Duncan. He convinces the doubting and suspicious Malcolm of his honesty and integrity.

The cruel murders of all the members of Macduff's family make him the focus of sympathy. He responds to the news of the murders with heroic fortitude, and emerges from the scene as the worthy champion of a good cause, and a formidable opponent of Macbeth.

THE WITCHES

WHEN Banquo asks the Witches what they are, he gets no answer. The play itself leaves their exact nature somewhat vague, and it is thus not possible to be dogmatic about the subject. Some commentators, however, have been in no doubt. A. C. Bradley was emphatic in his opinion that they are not goddesses, or fates, or supernatural beings of any kind. He was sure that Shakespeare had intended them as malicious, spiteful women who have acquired a limited range of supernatural powers from evil spirits. Banquo, however, a witness on the spot, has doubts about their humanity: their beards might well suggest to him that they are devils disguised as witches. Shakespeare's main source for the play, Holinshed, spoke of the Witches as 'goddesses of destiny' with the gift of prophecy. Some members of Shakespeare's audience might have thought of them as fates; 'Weird', the name he gives them, is derived from the Anglo-Saxon word for fate. It is possible that others saw them as Bradley did, simply as old women who practised witchcraft. In a fine essay on the play, Hazlitt makes a useful distinction between the flesh-and-blood display of passion by Lady Macbeth, and 'the cold, abstracted, gratuitous servile malignity of the Witches, who are equally instrumental in urging Macbeth to his fate for the mere love of mischief, and from a disinterested delight in deformity and cruelty'.

Their love of mischief is clear enough in Act I, Scene 3. One of them has vented her spite on the sailor's wife who refused her some chestnuts; another has killed her neighbour's swine, a particularly bloody operation. Their power to harm is, however, clearly restricted. They can prophesy, control the winds, and severely annoy a sailor, but they cannot kill him ('his bark cannot be lost').

THE 'INSTRUMENTS OF DARKNESS'

The Witches may be limited in their powers and even ludicrously childish in their spiteful vindictiveness, but they play a vital role in the working out of Macbeth's destiny. It is of considerable significance that Shakespeare introduces them at the opening of the play, since this establishes them as likely to have a major influence on the progress of events. It is a mistake, however, to think of the Witches as manipulating the characters of *Macbeth* at will, as mere puppets. They are evil, but they cannot create evil in others. What they can do is to tempt Macbeth to proceed with an evil course of action he has already thought about. They make prophecies, but they do not tell Macbeth how to go about making these come to pass. Their prophecies are morally neutral. The evil they purvey becomes actual for Macbeth only when he submits to it by an act of his own will. We cannot, in other words, apportion to them the major share of the blame for the fatal series of events Macbeth and his wife set in motion. Bradley is surely right when he suggests that while the influence of the Witches' prophecies on Macbeth is very great, 'it is quite clearly shown to be an influence, and nothing more'. Their prophecies are formidable moral challenges with which Macbeth, unlike Banquo, is unable to deal adequately. The main difference between him and Banquo is that Macbeth is not prepared to combat actively the threats posed by the 'instruments of darkness', whereas Banquo is.

The essential point about the part played by the Witches in the evolution of the tragedy is made by Macbeth, much too late for his own good, when the truth about the dubious nature of the prophecies at last dawns on him. Macduff exposes the double meaning of the prophecy concerning himself (5, 8, 13-6), and Macbeth realises that his powerful sense of security was based on the fraud and equivocation of the Witches. His hopes and his activities all turned on their quibbling pronouncements. His second interview (Act 4, Scene 1) seemed to make him absolutely safe, since the Witches laid down apparently impossible conditions for his downfall (a moving forest and a man not born of woman). But such seeming impossibilities have come to pass, and Macbeth, facing death, is at last ready to see what Banquo acknowledged from the beginning about the Witches: 'And be these juggling fiends no more believed,/That palter with us in a double sense' (5, 8, 19-20). But he cannot attribute all the blame for his predicament to their equivocations, since he has all along been only too willing to derive the meaning most favourable to himself from all they have told him.

Language and Imagery

SHAKESPEARE achieves his characteristic effects by means of *poetic* language. Some examples will make clear what is meant. Angus says of Macbeth:

> Now does he feel
> His secret murders sticking on his hands
>
> 5, 2, 16-7.

Here we are not merely told that Macbeth is suffering from pangs of conscience or that he is afraid. Instead, we are given an impressively concrete illustration of what it is *like* to be Macbeth at this point. 'Secret' suggests the attempts to conceal the murders. It is juxtaposed with an image which suggests that such attempts are futile: the blood won't go away; it persists in 'sticking' to his hands. This one of a long series of such images. It echoes Lady Macbeth's 'wash this filthy witness from your hand' (2, 2, 48); 'smear/The sleepy grooms with blood' (2, 2, 50-1); 'A little water clears us of this deed' (2, 2, 68), and 'all the perfumes of/Arabia will not sweeten this little hand' (5, 1, 44-5). In the same series we have Macbeth's 'Will all great Neptune's ocean wash this blood/Clean from my hand?' (2, 2, 61-2), and 'As they had seen me with these hangman's hands' (2, 2, 29). A further example of the use of *tactile* imagery to make a more effective dramatic point than plain statement could possibly do is found in the reference to Macdonwald: 'The multiplying villainies of nature/Do *swarm* upon him' (1, 2, 11-2, editor's italics). This evokes a picture of the man's vices swarming all over him like insects, or perhaps even the accumulation around him of swarms of villainous rebels. Macbeth's temptation when he has been greeted as Thane of Cawdor (1, 3, 130-42) is similarly presented with *concrete* force. The rhythms of the speech suggest the pounding heart knocking at his ribs. The thought of murder does more than elicit from him an abstract statement of his terror; instead, we have his appalled recognition that its 'horrid image doth unfix my hair'. We get the very *feel* of Macbeth's experience in what L. C. Knights has called 'the sickening see-saw rhythm' of 'This supernatural soliciting/Cannot be ill, cannot be good . . .' (1, 3, 130*ff.*).

There are many reasons why critics should want to explore imagery, particularly metaphor and simile, as a major avenue of access to the 'meaning', structure and effect of Shakespeare's plays. In many of the plays there are groups of related images, and in some we find single dominant image motifs: animal imagery in *King Lear,* images of disease, corruption and poison in *Hamlet,* images of disorder, false appearance and disease in *Macbeth.* This prevalence of recurring images has prompted critics to trace the thematic patterns which these images suggest.

IMAGES OF FALSE APPEARANCE

In *Macbeth* we find a number of image-patterns which help to express some of the major themes of the play. One of its most frequently-recurring ideas is that false appearance is inseparable from evil. This idea finds expression in a wide range of related images and non-figurative statements. Abstract statements on the prevalence of hypocrisy and deceit are very numerous. Duncan, having discovered Cawdor's treachery, moralises that 'There's no art/To find the mind's construction in the face' (1, 4, 11-2), while Malcolm, distrusting everyone after his father's murder, knows that 'To show an unfelt sorrow is an office/Which the false man does easy' (2, 3, 135-6). This commonplace is more effectively, because more concretely, expressed by Donalbain in 'There's daggers in men's smiles' (2, 3, 139). But the important images of disguise and concealment are used by, and in relation to, Macbeth. This is natural enough, since he acquires at the beginning, and maintains for a long time, the habit of deception. Indeed, his career is built on it. We are repeatedly reminded of his need to maintain a false appearance if his schemes are to succeed: 'To beguile the time,/Look like the time . . . look like the innocent flower,/But be the serpent under't (1, 5, 62-5); 'False face must hide what the false heart doth know' (1, 7, 82). It is significant that from this point until Act 4, when he drops all pretence at concealment, Macbeth employs the kind of masking images that have hitherto been a feature of his wife's speeches.

The use of this kind of imagery may be interpreted in various ways. Shakespeare may be understood to be showing us Lady Macbeth's ascendancy over her husband's mind. Macbeth's habit of using her kind of language betrays his readiness to learn from her. We may choose to see the free use of masking imagery as evidence that the practice of maintaining a false appearance before the world has become second nature to Macbeth. In his interview with the murderers he explains why he wants to be rid of Banquo without having to use barefaced power: certain friends whose support he finds necessary would react unfavourably, so he must resort to 'Masking the business from the common eye/For sundry weighty reasons' (3, 1, 125-6). In the earlier scenes it was Lady Macbeth who used the most memorable images of concealment. But by the time Macbeth has decided to have Banquo murdered without consulting his wife, it is he who takes the initiative in urging on her the need for dissimulation:

> Let your remembrance apply to Banquo;
> Present him eminence, both with eye and tongue —
> Unsafe the while, that we
> Must have our honours in these flattering streams,
> And make our faces vizards to our hearts,
> Disguising what they are
>
> 3, 2, 30-5.

This is reminiscent of Lady Macbeth's own advice to Macbeth before Duncan's murder (1, 5, 61-5) when he was encouraged to look like a flower but to be like a serpent. And in his final speech of Act 3, Scene 2, he longs for the 'seeling night' to come and 'Scarf up the tender eye of pitiful day', repeating almost exactly the night image used by both of them earlier (1, 5, 49*ff.*) and (2, 1, 49*ff.*). After the banquet scene, which has exposed his real character to the world, Macbeth uses fewer images of masking or conceal-ment. A turning-point is reached when he decides to take revenge on Macduff. From this moment, as he puts it, 'The very firstlings of my heart shall be/The firstlings of my hand' (4, 1, 147-8). The mask is finally off; there is no further point in disguise, and appearance and reality become one.

CLOTHING IMAGERY

The most interesting single image-pattern, certainly the one that has attracted most critical attention, is drawn from clothing. Garment metaphors and similes are introduced at crucial moments and given a special emphasis. The keynote of the series is struck by Macbeth. Having been greeted by Ross as Thane of Cawdor, he expresses his incredulity by means of an image of borrowed clothes: 'The Thane of Cawdor lives: why do you dress me/In borrowed robes?' (1, 3, 108-9). Soon afterwards, Banquo uses a similar image: the new honours bestowed on his partner are like strange garments which 'cleave not to their mould/But with the aid of use' (1, 3, 145-6). Later, at Inverness, Macbeth uses another clothing image to express his reluctance to murder Duncan. He has bought 'Golden opinions from all sorts of people,/Which would be worn now in their newest gloss,/Not cast aside so soon' (1, 7, 33-5). Lady Macbeth's reply develops the metaphor: 'Was the hope drunk/Wherein you dressed yourself?' The image reappears after the murder, when Macduff hints that the 'old robes' of Duncan's kingship may well sit easier than the new ones of Macbeth's (2, 4, 38). Angus was present when Banquo compared Macbeth's new honours to ill-fitting garments. As the invaders move towards Dunsinane, Angus seems to recall Banquo's image:

> now does he feel his title
> Hang loose about him, like a giant's robe
> Upon a dwarfish thief
>
> 5, 2, 20-2.

The recurrence of these images is not easy to dismiss as accidental, but differing opinions have been expressed as to its precise significance. Caroline Spurgeon, who first remarked on it, suggested that through it Shakespeare was depicting a petty, ignoble man snatching at power he was quite unfitted to possess. She found in the clothing images as a whole the imaginative picture of a man degraded by garments unsuited to him, kingship not being his proper role. However a later critic, Cleanth Brooks, finds the crucial point of the images not in the smallness of the man and the largeness of the robes, but in the fact that these are not Macbeth's garments; they are actually stolen. He is uncomfortable in them because they do not *belong* to him. The same critic argues that the clothing imagery fits into a larger pattern, the contrast between Macbeth and his garments being part of the wider contrast between appearance and reality.

VIOLENT, DARK IMAGERY

In addition to the groups of images which help to develop the main themes of the play, there are others which contribute to its distinctive mood or atmosphere. Large image-clusters combine to make the prevailing atmosphere of *Macbeth* one of gloom, evil and violence. Even when the blackness is relieved by flashes of colour, these have sinister associations, since the dominant colour is that of blood. The most memorable scenes are set in darkness. Duncan is murdered in his sleep; Banquo dies as 'Light thickens'. The two great speeches of ritual dedication to evil (1, 5, 39*ff.* and 2, 1, 49*ff.*) are full of images of darkness. After Duncan's murder, day turns to night.

The animal imagery of the play reinforces the impression of terror. Macbeth pictures the black agents of night rising to devour their prey as he plans Banquo's death. There are images of a 'hell-kite' eating chickens, a devouring vulture, a wren fighting for the life of its young, small birds fearing snares, horses eating each other, a bear tied to a stake fighting off savage dogs.

'Hell is murky', says Lady Macbeth during her sleepwalking scene. The association between evil and darkness is constantly in the imagery. The Witches are 'secret, black and midnight hags'. It is only in darkness that Macbeth can carry out his designs. Again, the symbolism is clear enough. It is also clear in the case of another recurring image. One industrious commentator pointed out that the play has over one hundred references to blood and its effects, which make this the dominant image. Blood is not merely the subject of figurative language. It is often a visual image: we see daggers, swords and hands covered in it. The bleeding officer rushes in calling for help for his wounds. Macbeth looks in horror at his bloody hand; Banquo's murderer presents himself with blood on his face; Banquo appears 'blood-boltered'. The deaths of Banquo, Macduff's son and young Siward are all enacted on stage; in the final scene Macduff enters with Macbeth's head. One can associate the recurring images of drunkenness with those of blood, and find in this association a clue to Macbeth's willingness to enact his original crime again and again. His craving for blood is like a drunkard's thirst for oblivion. And there can be no release, because each satisfaction merely intensifies the original need, and the only oblivion can be in bestiality.

One further group of atmospheric images is that conveying violence and rapid movement, appropriate in a play of tumult and disorder. The messenger arrives at Inverness gasping for breath. Macbeth outrides Duncan. There are many verbal images of violent motion in the play. Lady Macbeth talks of dashing out the brains of her smiling infant. The night of Duncan's death is rough and unruly. We hear of sorrows striking heaven in the face, of the mind being tortured as if stretched on a rack, of heaven's cherubim horsed on the storm, of Macbeth's deed being blown in every eye. Violence and disorder are evoked by Macbeth in the rhetoric of the cauldron scene (4, 1): 'Though you untie the winds and let them fight/ Against the churches . . .'

IMAGES OF GOODNESS, VIRTUE AND GRACE

To concentrate attention exclusively on the imagery of evil in *Macbeth* would be to falsify the imaginative impression created by the play. The imagery of moral darkness is counterbalanced to some extent by imagery of positive goodness, of virtue, grace and natural life. Duncan, for example, is associated with images of natural growth and fertility (Act 1, Scenes 4 and 6). It is significant that while Macbeth is associated with hell, the agents opposed to him are often presented in terms of religious symbols. This is best illustrated by reference to Act 3, Scene 6. Here the emphasis is repeatedly laid on images of grace and holiness, suggesting that Macbeth's enemies are supernaturally sanctioned, at least in their own eyes. Macduff has fled to 'the most pious Edward', the 'holy king' who has received Malcolm 'with such grace'. There are prayers for the aid of 'Some holy angel' for a 'swift blessing' on Scotland. God's aid is invoked and expected ('with Him above/To ratify the work'). The episode of the king's evil (4, 3, 141-59) reminds us that in *Macbeth* not all things are given over to disorder and destruction. This whole scene is remarkable for its density of religious images. One of these images involves a particularly appropriate contrast between the conflicting forces operating throughout *Macbeth:*

Angels are bright still, though the brightest fell.
Though all things foul would wear the brows of grace.
Yet grace must still look so

4. 3. 22-4.

DRAMATIC IMPORTANCE OF IMAGERY

It is useful and interesting to explore the thematic implications of
recurring images, but what of their *dramatic* importance? The most
profitable way to explore the significance of image-patterns in *Macbeth* is
to relate them to a stage performance. Consider, for example, the series of
images of ill-fitting clothes. In a performance, these images are much
more than *verbal:* they are made *visual* in the action. In his early
appearances Macbeth wears his armour, symbol of his warrior's nature
and achievements. When he defeats the Norwegians he is described as
being 'lapped in proof' (cased in strong armour). It is appropriate that we
should first see him dressed to suit the role for which he is so lavishly
praised. Then the early talk of 'borrowed robes' and 'strange garments'
finds *visual* expression in some form of royal, non-military dress, and even
in the nightgown he wears after Duncan's murder. From Act 2, Scene 3,
until Act 5, Scene 3, he is dressed in the borrowed robes of kingship, which
he wears uneasily. When he played Macbeth, the nineteenth-century actor
Edmund Kean wore a huge cloak entirely disproportionate to his slender
figure, thereby enforcing in visual terms what Angus says: 'now does he
feel his title/Hang loose about him, like a giant's robe/Upon a dwarfish
thief (5, 2, 20-2). But when the famous Garrick emerged after Duncan's
murder wearing a flowered dressing-gown, he was probably carrying the
visualisation of verbal images too far; he was, it seems, playing the
serpent under the flowered gown in accordance with Lady Macbeth's
advice: 'look like the innocent flower,/But be the serpent under't' (1, 5,
64-5).

Towards the end, when Shakespeare needs to suggest that some of
Macbeth's old virtues (courage, manliness, warlike prowess) have not
deserted him, he makes him assume his armour once more. The passage
with Seyton ('Give me mine armour . . . Pull't off, I say . . .' 5, 3, 33*ff.*)
dramatically underlines Macbeth's return to the only way of life he
understands and in which he seems at ease. It is for the actor to suggest

just how uneasy he feels in the assumed robes of monarchy, and how comparatively self-assured he is in his warrior's armour. The visual impact of his changes of costume finds an ironic parallel in Macduff's prophetic 'adieu!/Lest our old robes sit easier than our new!' (2, 4, 37-8).

All of this suggests that it is important to keep performance in mind when we are reading the play with a view to commenting on its imagery. Another instance of the close harmony maintained by Shakespeare between verbal images and visual ones is found in 5, 2, 15-6. Caithness declares that Macbeth 'cannot buckle his distempered cause/Within the belt of rule'. In the next scene, the truth of this saying is symbolically *enacted*. Much is made of Seyton's attempt to help Macbeth don his armour. There is a good deal of fumbling. Macbeth cannot put his armour on without difficulty; he is restless and impatient. 'Pull't off, I say', is addressed to Seyton, whose attempt to untie some band or other is interrupted by Macbeth's command to break it instead and bring it along after him. Caithness pictures Macbeth as a man no longer in full control of himself or of his destiny: in the stage-business with Seyton we have a visual representation of his frantic insecurity. Having heard that Malcolm's army is approaching, he calls three times for his armour, and then won't stay to put it on properly.

One further example of the way in which images come alive in performance is found in the following passage, and in the stage-business which must inevitably have accompanied it in Shakespeare's theatre. Similar stage-business is, of course, still possible in the modern theatre:

Macduff

> Awake! Awake!
> Ring the alarum-bell. Murder and treason!
> Banquo and Donalbain! Malcolm! Awake!
> Shake off this downy sleep, death's counterfeit,
> And look on death itself! Up, up, and see
> The great doom's image! Malcolm! Banquo!
> As from your graves rise up, and walk like sprites,
> To countenance this horror!
>
>   *[Bell rings.*
>
>   *Enter* Lady Macbeth

Lady Macbeth

> What's the business,
> That such a hideous trumpet calls to parley
> The sleepers of the house?

2, 3, 72*ff.*

Macduff is calling on the sleepers of Macbeth's house to arise and witness an image of Judgement Day, sleep being an image of death, and death a prelude to final judgement. But these verbal images are dramatically matched by visual ones, as the sleepers of the house, clad in night attire come on the stage by every entrance, probably using even the trapdoor, looking much like spirits rising from their graves on the Last Day, thereby impressively and eerily answering Macduff's 'As from your graves rise up, and walk like sprites'. Lady Macbeth's reference to the alarm-bell as a hideous trumpet reinforces the imagery of death and judgement.

Tragic Irony

THERE are various kinds of irony, but common to all is a contrast between appearance and reality, between what is said, suggested or thought on the one hand, and what is actually the case, on the other. The simplest kind of irony we encounter in *Macbeth* involves a clear and obvious contrast between what is said and what is meant. A good example of this is found in Act 3, Scene 6, where Lennox, in a heavy-handed way, pretends to accept Macbeth's version of events, and thereby manages to get in some bitter by-blows at his king: 'So that, I say,/He has borne all things well' (3, 6, 16-7).

From beginning to end, *Macbeth* is liberally interspersed with local ironies, and some larger ones. A pleasantly-situated castle, extravagantly admired by a king about to enter it as a guest, is the scene of that king's frightful murder, performed by the man whose guest he is. The same king continually hails as his benefactor the man who is about to murder him. The hostess says that her chief guest is about to be provided for when she means that he is to be murdered.

Shakespeare organises his ironies with consistent deliberation. The most powerful effects are achieved when a speaker, confident that things are as they seem, puts an interpretation on events which the knowing spectator is able to alter and correct. Many of the main characters of *Macbeth* are victims of this kind of irony. Time after time a speaker uses words which carry one kind of meaning for him or her, but a further, generally sinister, meaning for the audience. In the first scene, the Witches' creed is firmly stamped on our minds: 'Fair is foul, and foul is fair'. Macbeth's first words, 'So foul and fair a day I have not seen', are a startling reminder of what the Witches have said and carry ominous overtones for the audience.

The overall pattern of the play, particularly the working out of Macbeth's destiny, involves major tragic irony. This arises when a character acts in a manner quite inappropriate to his actual circumstances, or confidently expects the opposite of what fate holds in store for him. It also arises when he says something that anticipates the actual outcome, but not at all in the way that he means it. In *Macbeth* Shakespeare makes use of the irony of fate which means that the hero's destruction is the work of his own unwitting hands, of somebody (Lady Macbeth) who wishes him well, and of the Witches and Hecate whose promises and suggestions lead him on to false expectations. He thus works his way blindly to self-defeat. The main irony for Macbeth is the ambiguous nature of the Witches' prophecies on which he confidently relies for so long. He discovers their deceptiveness too late: 'And be these juggling fiends no more believed/ That palter with us in a double sense' (5, 8, 19-20). A major local irony is found in the scene where he goes to the Witches for reassurance: what he gets instead, without realising it, is a precise forecast of the manner of his defeat and death (Act 4, Scene 1). In all their proceedings, the two major characters are victims of this kind of irony. Lady Macbeth, who can contemplate the possibility of dashing out the brains of her own child (Act 1, Scene 7), is eventually hounded to death by the smell of Duncan's blood. Macbeth thinks that to gain a crown he would risk damnation in the next world, but finds that what he does to get and keep the same crown brings him all the horrors of damnation even in this life.

EXAMPLES OF IRONY

The following passages give an idea of the range of ironies in *Macbeth*.

1
> There's no art
> To find the mind's construction in the face:
> He was a gentleman on whom I built
> An absolute trust
>
> 1, 4, 11-4.

Duncan, chastened and saddened by Cawdor's treachery, is reflecting on how difficult it is to see beneath the outward appearances of people to the inner realities. The irony of this comment is immediately completed as Macbeth enters, to be greeted by Duncan as his 'worthiest cousin'. At this point *we* know, though of course Duncan does not, that Macbeth has been contemplating Duncan's murder. There is further irony in the same scene as Duncan confidently entrusts himself to Macbeth's keeping at Inverness, and, grimmest irony of all, tells him that, from the royal point of view, 'More is thy due than more than all can pay'. What Duncan is saying is that Macbeth deserves more than he can ever pay him. What he doesn't know is that from Macbeth's point of view his, Duncan's, life and his throne will be adequate rewards.

2
> Thy letters have transported me beyond
> This ignorant present, and I feel now
> The future in the instant
>
> 1, 5, 55-7.

The irony of Lady Macbeth's remark here resides in the contrast between the prosperous future she is contemplating for Macbeth and herself, and the terrible one which the events of the play will unfold. She doesn't for a moment anticipate the horrors which her actual transportation beyond the 'ignorant present' (another irony) will involve.

3   He that's coming
        Must be provided for; and you shall put
        This night's great business into my dispatch

                                                    1, 5, 65-7.

This is Lady Macbeth's response to Macbeth's news that Duncan is
to visit them. There is deliberate irony in these lines, understood as such
both by Lady Macbeth and her husband. 'Provided for' is a grim, ironic
pun. The explicit meaning is 'entertained', but the real, understood
meaning is 'murdered'. The pun is continued in 'dispatch', which means
both 'management' and 'execution'. Further depths of irony are revealed
when the lines are taken in conjunction with Lady Macbeth's speech
beginning 'The raven himself is hoarse' (1, 5, 37*ff*.). In that speech she has
asked the evil spirits to 'unsex' her. She will cast aside the normal role of
woman and hostess. Instead of providing for her unexpected guest in
terms of domestic comforts, she will provide for his death. It is this kind of
contrast that lends a terrible irony to these lines: 'That my keen knife see
not the wound it makes,/Nor heaven peep through the blanket of the dark'
(1, 5, 51-2). Here she is using the words 'knife' and 'blanket', which belong
to the domestic task of providing for a guest, as images of murder in
relation to the same guest. One of the layers of meaning in these lines is
that she is imagining stabbing the sleeping Duncan to death through a
covering blanket.

4   This castle hath a pleasant seat; the air
        Nimbly and sweetly recommends itself
        Unto our gentle senses

                                                    1, 6, 1-3.

Duncan is admiring the location of Macbeth's castle, the place where
he himself is soon to meet his death. In the light of what we have already
learned of Macbeth's intentions with regard to Duncan, these lines are
painfully ironic. We are only too aware how misplaced these happy
sentiments are. Further irony emerges if we read the lines with the
memory of Lady Macbeth's fatal resolutions still in our minds: 'The raven
himself is hoarse/That croaks the fatal entrance of Duncan/Under my
battlements' (1, 5, 37-9).

5 These deeds must not be thought
After these ways: so, it will make us mad

2, 2, 34-5.

Lady Macbeth is confronted by her overwrought husband; he is plagued by guilt and remorse after the murder of Duncan. As she speaks, it looks as if Macbeth is the one who is in danger of losing his sanity. It is she, however, whose mind will give way in the sleepwalking scene, which completes the irony of the piece of advice given above.

6 A little water clears us of this deed:
How easy is it then!

2, 2, 68-9.

This is Lady Macbeth's simple solution to all the problems confronting them both after Ducan's murder. She is to discover, of course, that there is no remedy for what she has set in train both for herself and for Macbeth. In the sleepwalking scene, she acknowledges in the depths of her being that nothing can purge her guilt: 'Here's the smell of the blood still: all the perfumes of/Arabia will not sweeten this little hand' (5, 1, 44-5).

7   O gentle lady!
'Tis not for you to hear what I can speak:
The repetition in a woman's ear
Would murder as it fell

2, 3, 82-5.

Lady Macbeth, with an impressive show of indignation, has enquired what 'business' could possibly be responsible for the rude awakening of the sleeping inhabitants of her house. Macduff, speaking in ignorance of the circumstances of Duncan's murder, is here the victim of the most extreme irony. Underlying this irony is the fact that Macduff has no idea of the nature of Lady Macbeth. If he had, he would not imagine that a description of the dead Duncan would prove fatal to her.

8 Had I but died an hour before this chance
I had lived a blessed time; for, from this instant,
There's nothing serious in mortality:
All is but toys; renown and grace is dead,
The wine of life is drawn, and the mere lees
Is left this vault to brag of

2, 3, 90-5.

This is Macbeth's public lament for Duncan, whom he has just murdered. The irony here is that he is, in fact, speaking the sober truth, although he intends his words to convey nothing but empty, hypocritical platitudes. The irony of this speech is completed in the 'Tomorrow' speech towards the end of the play (5, 5, 17-28) where he can declare, quite seriously, that life has become for him no better then a tale told by an idiot, 'Signifying nothing'.

9 Macbeth: Fail not our feast.
Banquo: My lord, I will not

3, 1, 28-9.

Both speakers are victims of irony here. Banquo is setting out on his journey in the happy assurance that he will be back in time for the royal banquet. He speaks in ignorance of his fate, and yet more wisely than he knows: he will not fail to turn up, although he will not appear at the banquet in human form. Macbeth is making what he imagines is a hypocritical farewell remark, little knowing that his chief guest will oblige him by turning up in a most unwelcome way.

Examining the Play

 A) FOR DETAILED DISCUSSION

ACT 1 • SCENE 1

1 What is to be learned from this scene about the extent of the Witches' powers?

2 Comment on the meaning and significance of the Witches' slogan: 'Fair is foul, and foul is fair'.

3 What is the function of the scene as a whole?

ACT 1 • SCENE 2

1 Duncan's opening question 'What bloody man is that?' is only one of the many references to blood and slaughter in this scene. Identify these references, and discuss their importance.

2 What do we learn about Macbeth's character in this scene?

3 Commentators have found the Captain's presentation of Macbeth somewhat disturbing. Do you find any reasons for this attitude?

4 Discuss the elements of language and imagery that make this a heroic scene.

ACT 1 • SCENE 3

1 This scene extends our knowledge of the nature of the Witches and of what they stand for. In what ways?

2 How is it suggested here that the powers of the Witches are limited?

3 Are the Witches to be taken with full seriousness as dangerous agents of evil and harm, or is there an element of childish mischief in their talk and activities?

4 There is a considerable difference between Macbeth and Banquo in their reactions to the Witches. Examine the difference, and account for it.

5   What is the significance of the message Ross brings concerning the fate of the Thane of Cawdor?

6   Is there anything surprising in Macbeth's reply to Ross, 'The Thane of Cawdor lives'? See the previous scene.

7   What do we learn of Banquo's character and motives from this scene?

8   It is sometimes argued that Macbeth is already a guilty man before he meets the Witches, that he has already thought seriously about the murder of Duncan. Does this scene confirm or, perhaps, contradict this impression?

9   To what extent do the Witches actually *tempt* Macbeth?

ACT 1 • SCENE 4

1   This scene contains some striking ironies. Examine the principal ones.

2   What impression of Duncan is conveyed in this scene?

3   Macbeth obviously has problems when he has to respond to Duncan's kindness and compliments. What are his problems? Is there any evidence that he is ill at ease?

4   Duncan's pronouncement 'We will establish our estate upon/Our eldest, Malcolm' is of vital importance to the entire plot. Explain.

5   Describe Macbeth's state of mind as revealed in his aside beginning 'The Prince of Cumberland . . .'

ACT 1 • SCENE 5

1   What exactly does Lady Macbeth think of her husband's character in her opening soliloquy? Why is she worried?

2   Do Lady Macbeth's impressions of her husband's character match those we get from the earlier scenes?

3   What do we learn about Lady Macbeth from her two soliloquies in this scene?

4   What is the relationship between husband and wife at this point in the play?

5   Deception, concealment and hypocrisy are key themes in the play. How are they conveyed in this scene?

6   The knife and blanket referred to by Lady Macbeth have more than one significance. Explain.

7   'He that's coming/Must be provided for'. What is implied here?

ACT 1 • SCENE 6

1   How would you describe the tone of the opening speeches of Duncan and Banquo?

2   This scene, like Act 1, Scene 4, is shot through with irony. Identify some examples.

3 Duncan is the central figure in this scene. What kind of impression does he make?

4 How would you describe Lady Macbeth's treatment of Duncan here? Compare her speeches with those of Macbeth to Duncan in Act 1, Scene 4. In what respect do the two sets of speeches differ?

ACT 1 • SCENE 7

1 Describe Macbeth's state of mind in his opening soliloquy.

2 Macbeth is making a strong case in this soliloquy. What is the nature of this case?

3 Macbeth is often described as a reluctant murderer. Does this soliloquy confirm this description? Explain.

4 Discuss the relationship between husband and wife in this scene.

5 This scene marks a considerable change in Macbeth's attitude to the killing of Duncan. How is this change brought about?

6 Lady Macbeth dominates this scene. How?

7 What outstanding qualities does Lady Macbeth display here?

ACT 2 • SCENE 1

1 The opening of the scene is tense and troubled. How is this impression conveyed?

2 Describe Banquo's state of mind in this scene.

3 How would you describe the Macbeth-Banquo relationship here?

4 Macbeth's soliloquy gives us a final glimpse of his mind before the murder. What does it reveal about his thoughts and feelings?

ACT 2 • SCENE 2

1 Contrast the attitudes of the two main characters in this scene.

2 How is Lady Macbeth's dominance suggested?

3 Describe the effects of the murder on Macbeth.

4 How would you describe Lady Macbeth's response to her husband's behaviour after the murder?

5 Can you think of anything earlier in the play that might have prepared us for Macbeth's outburst in this scene?

6 What is the significance of Macbeth's references to sleep?

7 What details suggest Macbeth's loss of control?

8 What is the dramatic significance of the knocking at the gate?

9 The scene as a whole is tense and exciting. In what ways?

ACT 2 • SCENE 3

1 Mention the elements in the Porter's speech that are relevant to the main themes of the play.
2 Why does the Porter imagine himself as porter of hell gate?
3 Does this scene give any hints of Macbeth's uneasiness?
4 What is the significance of the reports of unnatural events on the night of Duncan's murder?
5 Discuss Lady Macbeth's contribution to this scene.
6 How do you think the other participants in this scene feel about Macbeth's explanation of the murder of the chamberlains? Consider especially Banquo's likely feelings.
7 Is there any suggestion that Duncan's sons suspect Macbeth?

ACT 2 • SCENE 4

1 What are the main purposes of this scene?
2 What is the relationship between this scene and the previous one?
3 What do we learn about Ross from this scene?
4 Is there anything to suggest that Macduff is unhappy with Macbeth's version of the events surrounding Duncan's murder, or with Macbeth's accession to the throne? Contrast his attitude with that of Ross.
5 At the end of the scene there is a hint of trouble to come. Explain.

ACT 3 • SCENE 1

1 Banquo's soliloquy throws light on his thinking at this point. Explain.
2 Macbeth displays a new cunning in his dealings with Banquo. Give examples.
3 Compare Macbeth's soliloquy on Banquo ('To be thus is nothing . . .') with his earlier soliloquy on Duncan ('If it were done . . . Act 1, Scene 7).
4 Is Macbeth describing the prophecies of the Witches correctly in his soliloquy on Banquo? Refer back to Act 1, Scene 3.
5 There is evidence in Macbeth's interview with the murderers that his character has deteriorated. How does his present behaviour match Lady Macbeth's opinion of his character in Act 1, Scene 5, *ll.* 14 *ff.* ('Glamis thou art . . .')?
6 Is there any evidence in this scene that the relationship between Macbeth and Lady Macbeth may be changing?

ACT 3 • SCENE 2

1 What is the significance of the dialogue between Macbeth and Lady Macbeth at the beginning of this scene?

2 This scene marks a decisive change in the relationship between Macbeth and Lady Macbeth. Explain.

3 Macbeth's state of mind is clearly exposed in this scene. How would you describe it?

4 For many readers, Macbeth's final speech in this scene ('Be innocent of the knowledge . . .') recalls one of Lady Macbeth's earlier speeches ('The raven himself is hoarse . . .' Act 1, Scene 5, *ll.* 37 *ff*). Discuss the resemblances.

ACT 3 • SCENE 3

1 Comment on the significance of the third murderer.

2 Things go badly here for Macbeth. Why is the outcome of this scene so unfortunate for him?

ACT 3 • SCENE 4

1 What do Macbeth and Lady Macbeth hope to achieve from the state banquet?

2 The murderer supplies some graphic, gory details of Banquo's murder. In what way are these details important?

3 Macbeth's public reference to Banquo ('Here had we now our country's honour roofed . . .') is ironic. Explain.

4 Lady Macbeth tells her husband that his vision of Banquo is as much an illusion as 'the air-drawn dagger' of Act 2, Scene 1. Would you agree with her?

5 What is the effect of Macbeth's behaviour on his principal subjects here?

6 The appearance and re-appearance of the ghost have something in common with its two disappearances. What is this?

7 How would you describe Lady Macbeth's contribution to this scene? Mention some other episodes in the play where her intervention on Macbeth's behalf was also of critical importance.

8 How would you account for the obvious change in Lady Macbeth's manner and attitude after the guests have gone and when she is alone with Macbeth?

ACT 3 • SCENE 5

1 Does this scene suggest a new relationship between Macbeth and the Witches?

2 In the final lines of her speech ('He shall spurn fate . . .'), what does Hecate have in store for Macbeth? How is this prophecy fulfilled?

ACT 3 • SCENE 6

1   What is the tone of the opening speech of this scene?
2   The scene as a whole serves some important purposes. What are these?
3   The imagery of this scene is significant. In what ways?

ACT 4 • SCENE 1

1   What impressions of the Witches do we get from this scene?
2   What does Macbeth's speech ('I conjure you . . .') reveal about his state of mind?
3   Comment on Macbeth's understanding of what the apparitions stand for.
4   What do the three apparitions represent?
5   'From this moment/The very firstlings of my heart shall be/The firstlings of my hand'. What does this mean? Is it a new resolution on Macbeth's part?

ACT 4 • SCENE 2

1   In the opening lines of the scene Lady Macduff raises doubts about her husband's motives for leaving Scotland and his family. Do these doubts seriously affect your view of Macduff's character?
2   Does Ross appear to have changed his attitude to Macbeth?
3   What impression is conveyed by the exchanges between Lady Macduff and her son?
4   Some commentators feel that the child's talk detracts from the dignity and seriousness of this grim scene. Would you agree?
5   How do the events of this scene affect our view of Macbeth?

ACT 4 • SCENE 3

1   One critic has argued that the lengthy exchange between Malcolm and Macduff in this scene 'serves to emphasise the mistrust that has spread from the central evil of the play'. Elaborate on this idea.
2   What are Malcolm's motives in behaving as he does here? What does he hope to achieve?
3   What do Macduff's responses tell us about his character?
4   This scene serves as a commentary on the condition of Macbeth's Scotland. What does it tell us?
5   Malcolm attributes many vices to Macbeth. Is there evidence elsewhere in the play that he is as bad as he is presented here?
6   This scene presents various views on kingship, good and bad. Discuss these.
7   What is the significance of the short discussion of the English king (*ll.* 140-59)?

8   This scene marks a major turning-point in Macbeth's fortunes although he does not appear in it. Explain.

ACT 5 • SCENE 1
1   Comment on the symbolism in this scene.
2   Many of Lady Macbeth's comments refer to earlier episodes in the play. Identify these.
3   How do you respond to Lady Macbeth in this scene?
4   There is irony in the breakdown of Lady Macbeth's reason. Explain.
5   Comment on the significance of the Doctor's view that 'Unnatural deeds/Do breed unnatural troubles'. Is there any evidence to support this view here or elsewhere in the play?

ACT 5 • SCENE 2
1   How close to the truth is the picture of Macbeth given by his enemies in this scene?
2   What are the implications of the various strands of imagery in this scene?

ACT 5 • SCENE 3
1   Our response to Macbeth in this scene is bound to be a divided one. Explain.
2   What is the effect of the lines beginning: 'my way of life . . .'?
3   How would you describe Macbeth's changing moods in this scene?

ACT 5 • SCENE 4
1   Malcolm's order to the soldiers to hew down the boughs of Birnam wood has major significance. Explain.
2   Malcolm and Macduff have different approaches to coming events. Explain.

ACT 5 • SCENE 5
1   In this scene, Macbeth is the dominant figure, the focus of intense interest. How is this interest created?
2   What is the tone of Macbeth's first speech here?
3   Consider Macbeth's second speech ('I have almost forgot the taste of fears . . .') as a commentary on his career.
4   What does the speech beginning 'She should have died hereafter . . .' reveal about the state of Macbeth's mind at this point?

5   As in the previous scene, Macbeth goes through significant changes of mood.
      Explain.

ACT 5 • SCENES 6 AND 7

1   What does Scene 6 suggest about Malcolm's position?
2   How do you respond to Macbeth's short speech at the beginning of Scene 7?
3   What is Macbeth's mood after he has killed young Siward?

ACT 5 • SCENES 8 AND 9

1   Describe Macbeth's varying moods in Scene 8.
2   How does Shakespeare wish us to see Macbeth as his death approaches? How
      does he achieve this?
3   Malcolm talks about Macbeth and Lady Macbeth as 'this dead butcher and
      his fiend-like queen'. Is this a fair and reasonable summary of their
      characters as we have known them from the beginning?
4   Discuss the implications of 'fiend-like' as applied to Lady Macbeth.

B) FOR GENERAL DISCUSSION

1   It is impossible to read *Macbeth* without being impressed by its repeated emphasis on the prevalence of evil forces in its world.

2   In *Macbeth,* the sympathies of the audience are gradually switched from the hero to his enemies.

3   Throughout the play, appearance is contrasted with reality.

4   The play has a great deal to say about contrasting ideas of kingship.

5   In *Macbeth,* a noble character is entirely overpowered by mysterious, inexplicable temptation.

6   Macbeth struggles dreadfully against his own nature, and wins the terrible victory of his damnation.

7   Lady Macbeth is a sprinter in evil; her husband, slower to get off the mark, is the long-distance runner.

8   The imprisoning fantasy of his ambition keeps Macbeth at arm's length from everyone except his wife until, as he goes deeper into crime they draw apart, each dying, as they had come to live, in loneliness.

9   To talk of *Macbeth* as dramatising a conflict between good and evil is to simplify too much.

10 Darkness and blindness are major themes in *Macbeth.*

11 Lady Macbeth's major problem is how to get her husband to act against his own nature.

12 In *Macbeth,* Shakespeare expresses Christian ideas on all the major issues.

13 Seen in terms of its major events, *Macbeth* is a particularly horrific crime story. Shakespeare's treatment of his themes and characters, however, makes it much more than this.

14 The sleepwalking scene is a dream-like re-enactment of what has gone before.

15 In *Macbeth* Shakespeare makes extensive use of parallels and contrasts between characters, themes, situations and incidents. Irony plays a significant part in all of these.

16 The relationship between Macbeth and his wife undergoes significant changes in the course of the play.

17 It is not Macbeth's enemies who excite our imaginations, but Macbeth himself, as he gives us one glimpse after another of his tortured state of mind.

18 Lady Macbeth, for all her wickedness, arouses some sympathy. She is not, what Dr. Johnson claimed she is, 'merely detested'.

19 The Witches play a significant part in the events of *Macbeth,* but their influence is not decisive.

20 Macbeth becomes a villain, but he never entirely loses our sympathy because we feel and suffer with him.

Critical Comment

1 Lady Macbeth is merely (completely, absolutely) detested; and though the courage of Macbeth preserves some esteem, yet every reader rejoices at his fall.

Samuel Johnson

2 Lady Macbeth, like all in Shakespeare, is a class individualised — of high rank, left much alone, and feeding herself with daydreams of ambition, she mistakes the courage of fantasy for the power of bearing the consequences of the realities of guilt. Hers is the mock fortitude of a mind deluded by ambition; she shames her husband with a superhuman audacity of fancy which she cannot support, but sinks in the season of remorse, and dies in suicidal agony.

S. T. Coleridge

3 The magnitude of her resolution almost covers the magnitude of her guilt. She is a great bad woman, whom we hate, but whom we fear more than we hate. She is only wicked to gain a great end; and is perhaps more distinguished by her commanding presence of mind and inexorable self-will, which do not suffer her to be diverted from a bad purpose, when once formed, by weak and womanly regrets, than by the hardness of her heart or want of natural affections.

William Hazlitt

4 Macbeth's deed is done in horror, and without the faintest desire or sense of glory — done, one may almost say, as if it were an appalling duty; the instant it is finished, its futility is revealed to Macbeth as clearly as its vileness had been revealed beforehand.

A. C. Bradley

5 Macbeth has staked everything and lost; he has damned himself for nothing; his world suddenly turns into a blank of imbecile futility. Tragedy can lay hold of no evil worse than the conviction that life is an affair of absolute inconsequence. There is no meaning anywhere; that is the final disaster; death is nothing after that.

Lascelles Abercrombie

6 The antithesis between the two Macbeths is that between the practical life and the intellectual, and the effects of this difference are everywhere apparent. Macbeth is bold and resolute in the moment of action; he can kill a king, and he has a curious gift of ready speech throughout. But when there is nothing to be done, he is devoid of self-control; he cannot wait nor stand still; he becomes prey to countless terrible imaginings; he is wildly superstitious. Of all this Lady Macbeth is the exact converse. She has banished superstition from her soul. She is strong enough of will to quell her husband's cowardly fears. She can scheme and plot, but she cannot act. She must leave the actual doing of the deadly deed to Macbeth. At the moment of discovery she faints.

E. K. Chambers

7 *Macbeth* defines a particular kind of evil — the evil that results from a lust for power.

L. C. Knights

8 In *Macbeth,* evil is, for once and without doubt, larger, more fascinating, more effective than the pallid representation of good.

C. K. Hunter

9 The close of *Macbeth* shows deadly ironic justice. Macbeth and his wife expel pity and remorse from their natures, and they find themselves confronted by a world that has no pity for them.

Helen Gardner

10 At the end, political order is restored, and universal coherence re-established, with a beneficent Providence triumphant. All things needful for a regenerated Scotland, Malcolm will perform.

G. I. Duthie

11 The action of a tragedy must end in disaster. More than a bare hint of the rebirth or renewal theme is dangerous. A production of *Macbeth* which allowed all our sympathy for Macbeth to ebb before the desperate scenes of Acts 4 and 5, and encouraged us to identify ourselves and our interests with Malcolm, would transform the play into a melodrama.

Roy Morrell

12 Macbeth is a perfectly reasonable ordinary man driven by a comprehensible ambition. He is impelled by his own ambition and by forces outside him towards an object, the Crown, which is well within his grasp. Having reached the top, however, he finds that it means nothing.

Eric Porter, the actor

13 Macbeth is no moral monster, but a sensitive and able man driven by an obsession with an unexamined ambition to do what he knows to be evil and what at first his whole nature shrinks from. Of course he becomes bloodier as he proceeds, for that is the nature of crime, but the real tragedy lies in the meaninglessness of his ambition almost as soon as it is achieved, and his determination to carry on and pay over and over again the price of what he knows is worthless.

David Daiches

14 Macbeth's tragic career is threefold. He does not understand the two forces working on him from the outside, he does not understand the difference between 'bloody execution' in civilian and military life, and he does not understand his own character. He does not understand what will be the effect of the act on his own future happiness.

Wayne Booth

15 Neither Macbeth nor Lady Macbeth shows any sign of repentance, and one of the dramatist's major problems was to prevent their being the monstrous figures of evil they seem to their enemies. His method was to insist, as so often before, on the mixed nature of human beings, and by entering into their minds and letting them express their doubts and revulsions, to suggest that their evil behaviour was a wasteful misdirection of energy which might easily have been turned to good; so he preserves a modicum of sympathy for them even at their worst moments. He presents the paradox that however much Macbeth and Lady Macbeth try to dehumanise themselves, they cannot entirely do so.

Geoffrey Bullough

16 In *Macbeth* Shakespeare seems more interested in general ideas than in historical accuracy or particularity of characterisation. Many of the characters are purely functional. Duncan is primarily a symbol of the values that Macbeth is to overthrow. He is counterbalanced by the equally generalised Weird Sisters. Even Banquo figures mainly as a measure of the norm from which Macbeth deviates. The Witches, with their incantations, spells and grotesque rituals, suggest evil as a universal force which can be tapped and channelled through human agents.

Stanley Wells

17 *Macbeth is* a study of two characters whose finest quality, their mutual love, becomes under evil ambition the means of their ruin. Nothing is more poignant than the interplay of influence between Macbeth and his wife. Without the other, neither would have sinned, for Macbeth's exorbitant ambition has plenty of natural checks and balances, and her urgency in crime is so wholly altruistic and uncomprehending as to be almost virtuous.

M. A. Shaaber

18 Sir Lawrence Olivier's Macbeth is paralysed with guilt before the curtain rises, having already killed Duncan time and again in his mind. Far from recoiling and popping his eyes, he greets the air-drawn dagger with sad familiarity; it is a fixture in the crooked furniture of his brain.

Kenneth Tynan

19 The key to Lady Macbeth's actions is that she has no imagination. A blinkered, fiercely acquisitive woman, she has no eyes for anything except the golden prize that seems to have fallen within her grasp. She never lifts her head to the horizon. As she trots around busily making preparations for the murder, drugging the grooms' drink, laying out the daggers, arranging this or contriving that, she has no time to think what she is really doing; she is satisfied to keep one jump ahead of the action.

John Wain

20 It is going too far to believe that the Witches are embodiments of evil. The real evil, the truly terrifying things, are to be found not in the Weird Sisters or in the quaint revelations of Ross and the Old Man, but in the speeches of Macbeth and Lady Macbeth. Evil in the play is largely what Macbeth does to himself.

D. J. Enright